Redemptive Compassion®
Making a Defining Difference

Includes *The Wagon Principle*

Lois M. Tupyi

"I am for doing good to the poor, but I differ in opinion of the means. I think the best way of doing good to the poor, is not making them easy in poverty, but leading or driving them out of it. In my youth I travelled much, and I observed in different countries, that the more public provisions were made for the poor, the less they provided for themselves, and of course became poorer. And, on the contrary, the less was done for them, the more they did for themselves, and became richer."

—Benjamin Franklin

Copyright © 2012, Lois M. Tupyi.

Second printing, 2017.

Redemptive Compassion®

Scripture taken from the HOLY BIBLE,
NEW INTERNATIONAL VERSION®. NIV®.
Copyright © 1973, 1978, 1984 by International
Bible Society. Used by permission of Zondervan.
All rights reserved worldwide.

⇥ Contents ⇤

7 Acknowledgments
8 Preface
11 Introduction

Redemptive Compassion

15 Week One: Imprisoned With Kindness
19   Day 1: Transforming Relationships
22   Day 2: Need-focused Giving
25   Day 3: Giving a Hand-Up
28   Day 4: Charity Compassion
31   Day 5: Developmental Compassion
34   Week One Study Application

39 Week Two: The Call to Love: Is It Possible?
42   Day 1: Does Poor Planning Beget Poor Stewardship?
45   Day 2: Imprisoned in Need
48   Day 3: Crippling Help
51   Day 4: Self-Serving or Sacrificial?
54   Day 5: Does It All Come Down to Love?
57   Week Two Study Application

62 Week Three: Seeing Through Our Father's Eyes
65   Day 1: God's Value System
68   Day 2: One Common Thread
71   Day 3: The Art of Listening
74   Day 4: Reflecting the Image of Our Creator
77   Day 5: Daring To Dream Again
80   Week Three Study Application

Contents

85	Week Four: Tough Love for Tough Times
89	Day 1: The Domino Effect
92	Day 2: Collective Spiritual Discernment
95	Day 3: Speaking the Truth in Love
98	Day 4: Choices and Consequences
101	Day 5: But I Need It!
104	Week Four Study Application
109	Week Five: Healing from the Inside Out
113	Day 1: About Our Father's Business
116	Day 2: Engaging Those We Serve
119	Day 3: I Must Do Something
122	Day 4: Raising Up a Child
125	Day 5: Fruit From Our Labor
128	Week Five Study Application
133	Week Six: Changing the World One Life at a Time
137	Day 1: Life Is Hard
140	Day 2: What's In Your Hand?
143	Day 3: Value of Work
146	Day 4: An Attitude of Gratitude
149	Day 5: We Are Not the Final Answer
152	Week Six Study Application
158	Conclusion
161	Summary

Contents

The Wagon Principle

171	Preface
172	Hope For a Better Life
173	Narcissa Whitman
175	The Wagon's Undercarriage
177	The Wagon Wheel
179	The Spiritual Wheel
181	The Physical/Material Wheel
183	The Relational/Social Wheel
185	The Emotional/Self Wheel
187	The Wagon Box
189	The Wagon Covering
191	The Wagon Train
193	Leading the Way
195	Pulling the Wagon Forward
197	Stages in the Journey
198	Stage One: Engage the Head
199	Stage Two: Engage the Heart
200	Stage Three: Engage the Hands and Feet
201	Summary of the Map to Success
203	A Transformed Life
204	A Pictorial Description
205	In Closing
206	Testimonials
207	About the Author

Acknowledgments

My heartfelt gratitude goes to:

Craig Eshelman: He was the first to suggest this should be written, providing ongoing support, redirection, and encouragement as it took on life. Thank you for challenging me with honest, constructive insight that kept me centered on the audience and focused on the purpose of the book.

Gwyneth Bledsoe: Her unending prayerful editing and thought-provoking comments kept me reworking each concept into clear and concise thoughts that helped make the finished product more palatable to the reader.

Renee Howe: Her ability to see things through the lens of her life journey brought a depth of understanding and an enriched perspective I would have missed without her insight.

Debbie Eshelman: Her research and knowledge of words helped make the book viable and relevant to the readers of this generation

Terry and Gayellen Smith: The husband and wife editing team who painstakingly tightened up the verbiage, adding the professional touch needed to produce a quality product.

Test Pilot Study Group: Lloyd Ayers, Gwyneth Bledsoe, Nancy Daniels, Craig Eshelman, Hilary Ford, Grant Henry, Renee Howe, and Rick Irish who, together, test-piloted the six week study guide draft, offering valuable insight as I refined the final copy.

My Husband, Basil: God's gift to me as I daily learn invaluable insights by sharing life with someone who views the world differently, helping me stretch and grow each budding thought until it bursts forth into new life.

Love INC Family: The Love INC Leadership Board, staff and countless friends who believed it was important to share the *Redemptive Compassion* principles with others. Without their constant support, encouragement and prayers this book would not exist.

⇥ Preface ⇤

"The words I say to you are not just my own. Rather, it is the Father, living in me, who is doing His work." —John 14:10

An anxious anticipation unsettled my spirit the first time I spoke publicly about the philosophy of *Redemptive Compassion* even though it had been years in the making. As I stood at the podium, unsteady hands and shaking voice, I knew my life would never be the same after this night—and it hasn't been.

The revelations I felt led to share were birthed out of my intense struggle with a standard I found unacceptable. In their infancy, newly-formed thoughts and words scrambled together in disjointed pieces like a broken puzzle. Over time, as I worked with more and more people in need, the pieces started to fit together to show a reality that confused and saddened me. How could such good intentions have become so ineffective and destructive? With so many entities, organizations and individuals attempting to help people in need, why did the commonly-used methods seem so ineffective in reducing or alleviating ongoing need for those served? Could this crippling lifestyle that thousands of individuals and families were trapped in be all God had planned for them? Or had something sabotaged their future hopes, replacing them with indifference and complacency, which fostered a sense of entitlement and bleak acceptance of what appeared to be their destiny? The answer to these and so many other questions drove me to my knees as I sought audience with God to discern truth. As I relentlessly pushed forward into His Word I realized the answers would be difficult to share but impossible to hide. This passion God was igniting in me could not be contained and I found it shaping everything about me—my priorities and the ministry I led. I was at a crossroads in my life and, out of obedience, chose to follow God. For me, these questions begged for an answer—How are we called to do Kingdom work on earth? Why have our good intentions produced such devastating results?

I find myself an unlikely candidate to approach such a broad and contro-

Preface

versial topic, lacking formal credentials on the subject. But what I do have is an unquenchable thirst to know truth as God reveals it and years of hands-on experience, interacting with hundreds of people living in need situations. I believe I have only scratched the surface of knowledge in this area and almost daily learn something new on the subject. But over the course of the last few years I have felt a need to share with others what I'm learning so they too can struggle through the biblical principles and precepts God is working out in me. My passion to understand and share how we are called to help people in a godly way has been the driving force behind this study guide.

Putting my thoughts on paper has been challenging. The format and content of the book has developed over time. A team of individuals I respect and trust have helped me formulate the concepts into a form that promotes personal study and growth while giving practical tools to help apply what is learned. The topic of addressing need evokes emotions within all of us. The questions must be wrestled with privately and individually, but require a final consensus within a larger group if the answers are to be fully embraced and implemented with those we seek to help. The intent of the study guide is not to give a final or expert answer on each concept, but to move the reader into further contemplation with God and others on what we are biblically called to do when addressing need. I have faith that the Holy Spirit will affirm truth to anyone seeking it and this truth will bring clarity and light to a confusing and multi-faceted topic.

My personal expertise comes from working in a local mission field as the Executive Director of a non-profit Christian ministry called Love In the Name of Christ (Love INC). Our purpose is to unite individuals attending Christian churches within a geographic area and mobilize them to serve through defined and organized service opportunities that meet legitimate individual and family needs. The core of what we do and how we do it is designed to promote transformation within those being served as well as

Preface

those performing the service. It is through my experience with my local affiliate, Love INC of Treasure Valley, and my position as a trainer and leader within the movement of Love INC nationally that I have witnessed and wrestled with the concepts laid out in the study guide.

I encourage each reader to seriously embrace this critical subject and to seek truth as only God can give. Before I began writing I reread the complete Bible pulling out and categorizing every Scripture that referred to need, healing and wholeness in life. It is important to me that each concept be supported with Scripture so it can be prayerfully and earnestly studied, discerning what God says on the subject. My personal prayer is that anyone who reads and studies this guide will be challenged and forever changed. What could change in our nation and around the world if we changed how we address need so that it changed the lives and future of those we serve? We individually hold the key to this answer. Let us together seek truth and, once learned, have the courage to walk in it.

"Now to Him who is able to do immeasurably more than all we ask or imagine, according to His power that is at work within us, to Him be glory in the Church and in Christ Jesus throughout all generations, for ever and ever! Amen." —Ephesians 3:20&21

Introduction

I gripped the steering wheel tightly, fighting back the tears that seemed relentless. I had just finished another night of interviewing prospective clients for our long-term relational programs and was headed home, but my emotions were raw and I welcomed the time alone with God. The last interview had been difficult and had left me questioning myself and my role as the Director of our non-profit. The angry words hurled at me by the husband of the couple I was interviewing had hit deep inside me as I hauntingly contemplated "who did I think I was and what was I doing?" I had challenged his denial of being addicted to prescription drugs, staying firm in my position until he broke down and admitted he needed help. But now, alone in the car with only God to hear me, my mind replayed his accusations, insults and hurtful words. My education of dealing with people in need had come from field experience, not from a classroom. I knew God had called me into this ministry of helping others but I came without experience or formal training. It wasn't what I had initially expected, and I realized early on that the popular methods of assisting others weren't bringing about the necessary life changes required to move people out of need. My lack of experience kept me on my knees and in God's classroom. My greatest strength was my awareness that in my weakness God would prove sufficient, and He had. But tonight I found myself questioning once again the role I felt God was asking me to play. Accepted methods for addressing need just didn't seem to line up with what God was teaching me. Paving a new road in unfamiliar territory was difficult to say the least. God was calling me to something I had not sought, but a role I believed He had chosen me for. As I pulled into my driveway I prepared myself for another long night of praying and listening for His direction in this unfamiliar place I consistently found myself in. God was working out something in me that wasn't mine to keep. I knew the valuable secrets I was learning in the dark I would one day be asked to share. As I opened the door to my home the question resurfaced, "who was I and what was I doing?

I felt God's call to enter into fulltime ministry in 1993 but it took six long years before He placed me, using those years to prepare me for the foreign field of local mission work. I am a life-long student of my Lord but learned

Introduction

quickly that doing His work would require my relationship with Him to mature and deepen beyond what I could ever have imagined.

It didn't take me long to realize that need in America was crippling our nation, but not in the way one might suppose. I found few people physically dying from lack of daily essentials, yet they did seem to be starving for the full and productive life God desires for all of us. Many of the current helping efforts seemed to further complicate or contribute to the need-situation instead of solving it. generational poverty—people living in need for more than one generation—had now extended to the third and fourth generations within families. This lifestyle of dependency on others to survive seemed to be mushrooming uncontrollably as it was taught and passed from one generation to the next with little hope of change in sight. As I contemplated what God had planned for those struggling in need, the questions started coming but the answers I heard from God didn't seem familiar to many in the helping community.

If we want to see poverty change, we must change how we see poverty.

I believe one of the greatest challenges the Church faces when addressing people in need is a lack of education on the topic. This study guide is designed to provide an educational tool that can be used individually, through group study, or by an entire church body. Its purpose is to help those of us who feel called to assist others, biblically study and wrestle with what God has called us to do when addressing need in our communities. Need in America is not only on the increase but it is changing. Multitudes of people find themselves living on the edge and even the slightest hiccup has the potential to throw them off the cliff. If we want to see poverty change, we must change how we see poverty. It is a complicated subject because we are complex people. The face of poverty is multi-faceted and spans age, gender, and status.

⊰ Introduction ⊱

As I prayed about what God wanted me to do with what He was teaching me, I realized I didn't need to have all the answers. I needed to ask the right questions causing the reader to consider with God what the answers might be. As I've publicly spoken these insights, the Holy Spirit has been faithful to affirm in others the same things He's been teaching me. I believe God wants me to pass on these insights to you for your own thoughtful contemplation of this complex subject.

This six-week study begins each week with a fictional case story drawn from real life experiences. The names and details have been changed to protect the individuals. Within each week there are five individual studies which include a key concept, Scripture references, a case study application, and thought-provoking questions to ponder. The group study application at the end of the week should be done individually, but has also been designed to further explore and share personal beliefs and questions with other participants as a group. If the church is participating as a whole, the pastor may tie the sermon topic to the theme for the week.

My hope is to stimulate thought and conversation surrounding what we are biblically called to do when helping others. When status quo methods become ineffective or unacceptable, we will usually consider change. Living out the biblical concepts as God reveals them will probably involve change. While I firmly believe God's Church can and should meet need differently, the greater question is will it? This question must be answered individually, but will be corporately lived out through the church and community as a whole. Will we remain a contributor to the growing need-population or will we choose to become a major player in the solution? To answer the question of how and what we are called to do we must first understand what God says on the subject. Hebrews 4:16 instructs us "Let us therefore come boldly to the throne of grace, that we may obtain mercy and find grace to help in time of need." God is calling us to come to Him, for He is

Introduction

the only real source of wisdom and only He can show us how to live out compassion in ways that are redemptive.

Times are changing in America and I believe the church will soon be looked at as a valuable resource to address need. Government programs and resources are becoming more stretched and inadequate. There seems to be a growing realization that entities outside government can effectively do more than they can and it is opening doors for expanded church involvement. Will we be ready when the time comes? And more importantly, will we understand what God has biblically called us to do when the opportunity arises? When the Lord says, *"Whom shall I send and who will go for us?"* Will we hear and be ready to say, *"Here I am. Send me?"* Isaiah 6:8

"Those whom I love I rebuke and discipline. So be earnest, and repent. Here I am! I stand at the door and knock. If anyone hears my voice and opens the door, I will go in and eat with him, and he with me. To him who overcomes, I will give the right to sit with me on my throne, just as I overcame and sat down with my Father on His throne. He who has an ear, let him hear what the Spirit says to the churches." —Revelation 3:19–22

Week One:
Imprisoned with Kindness

Week One: Imprisoned with Kindness

Case Study Story

Steve was discouraged. He got up early because he wanted to be at the front of the line, but his car wouldn't start. By the time he finally got the engine to turn over, he had lost an hour. The frustration he felt toward the local mechanic, who was unwilling to work on his car without money up front, fueled his anger helping to ward off the frigid morning air. At least thirty people had beaten him to the front of the line and three times that many lined up behind him with more still coming. Some sat in chairs against the outer wall while others clustered together talking about nothing in particular. Steve stood aloof, blowing into his gloveless hands, and kicking the empty boxes lying at his feet. He wondered what would be left when it was his turn to walk to the tables strewn with food. Just his luck to have car trouble this morning, yet he knew it was a stroke of luck it had started at all. The car was on its last legs, unreliable and temperamental, not unlike Steve's own mood lately. "How many years have I been coming to these food banks?" he mumbled under his breath. A small boy playing with a ball caught his eye and his own childhood memories rushed to the surface. He could see himself in that child, innocent, yet keenly aware that if they didn't get a full box of food, supper would be slim that night. Steve couldn't remember when life hadn't been a daily struggle. His father never had consistent work. The angry words late at night between his parents used to wake him up. They moved a lot, unable to pay rent and utilities. The cold and sparsely furnished places seldom felt like home. His mother always seemed sad and preoccupied, frequently calling churches to find someone to help pay the bills and angry that people didn't help them more. The highlight each month was the day they got their food stamps. The whole family would go to the store and buy what they wanted—almost like Christmas. But the stamps never lasted long and standing in line for food was what they did to get by. He thought it would be different when he grew up but it wasn't. Like his father, he couldn't find a job he could keep. His wife had left him. His only son, also struggling to get by, only came around when he needed help. Sometimes Steve wondered if things would

Week One: Imprisoned with Kindness

Case Study Story

ever change, but he didn't think about it for long. This was all he knew. It was how his grandparents and parents had lived, so he believed it should be good enough for him too. But deep down he wondered why it wasn't different and the old feelings of shame crept to the surface. Shivering, he turned his back on the passing traffic, feelings of failure leaving him colder than the icy morning air.

Week One: Imprisoned with Kindness

Introduction

I didn't have to work in the ministry of Love INC[1] very long to be aware of one common and repeated pattern. Most people who called us for help had been experiencing chronic need for years. Their need might change from time to time, but the reality was their need defined their lives. Their struggle to survive and provide for their families was ongoing. I too have had seasons in my life when I experienced great need. But for me they were seasons, not a lifestyle. What makes the difference? Why are so many people trapped in places of poverty and reliant on others to help them survive? As I was pondering this, Isaiah 61:1&3 hit at the core of my heart,

> **Does it seem almost criminal that people can become imprisoned in their need?**

"*The Spirit of the Sovereign Lord is on me, because the Lord has anointed me to preach good news to the poor. He has sent me to bind up the brokenhearted, to proclaim freedom for the captives and release for the prisoners…to bestow on them a crown of beauty instead of ashes, the oil of gladness instead of mourning, and a garment of praise instead of a spirit of despair.*" It seems almost criminal that people can become imprisoned in their need, unable to escape without help. This week we will focus on what has contributed to this dilemma.

---

[1] Love in the Name of Christ

Week One: Imprisoned with Kindness

DAY ONE: Transforming Relationships

The giving of things can impact a life, but seldom transforms the individual. While things can change circumstances or situations, my personal experience has shown it takes a long-term relationship to truly see transformation in a person. If we want to substantially impact the lives of those we serve, isn't it as important to give of ourselves as the things they ask for? According to the dictionary, a transforming relationship is "a connection or bond between two or more individuals that has the capacity to alter or change a person." God is relational and He instructs us to enter into a relationship with Him and our fellow man, but for what purpose? Why are relationships foundationally important in Christianity? Could it be that agape love, defined as a love that is wholly selfless and spiritual, can only be expressed through a relationship? Does it take a relational bond to see change or transformation in an individual? And without a relationship is it possible to meet needs but leave the person untouched? Compassion is not just meeting a physical need, but being physically present in someone's time of need. Showing compassion means we are willing to feel and share their pain. Could it be that we show pity when we only focus on the need and express compassion when we also focus on the person?

Challenge: How important is it to develop a relationship with those we help?

⌗ Week One: Imprisoned with Kindness ⌗

DAY ONE: Transforming Relationships

SCRIPTURE REFERENCES

"All this is from God, who reconciled us to himself through Christ and gave us the ministry of reconciliation: that God was reconciling the world to Himself in Christ, not counting men's sins against them. And He has committed to us the message of reconciliation. We are therefore Christ's ambassadors, as though God were making His appeal through us. We implore you on Christ's behalf: Be reconciled to God."
—2 Corinthians 5:18–20

"Jesus went up into the hills and called to Him those He wanted, and they came to Him. He appointed twelve—designating them apostles—that they might be with Him and that He might send them out to preach."
—Mark 3:13&14

According to Scripture we are called to serve in ways that are redemptive. Jesus knew the importance of developing a close relationship with those He had chosen to carry on His work. The twelve left all they had and followed Him as He taught and mentored them over the course of a few years. The transformational work needed in each of their lives was not possible outside a close and personal relationship. God wants each of us to be reconciled to Him. Can building a relationship with someone potentially help them reconcile their relationship with God also?

Week One: Imprisoned with Kindness

DAY ONE: Transforming Relationships

CASE STUDY Steve had never known a life without need. He was taught the lifestyle of relying on others for assistance from early childhood. Continuing to have others meet his basic physical needs had not, and would not, change his overall situation. If Steve wanted to live differently, it would require someone willing to enter into a close and trusting relationship with him. Through this relationship different lifestyle choices, common and familiar to many but foreign and unknown to Steve, could be taught and modeled.

1. Is personal transformation possible without some type of relational component?

    No.

2. What emotions might a person feel when a physical need is met, but the relational connection is not made?

    They are not truly valued

3. What key relational components, if put into place, could make a difference in Steve's situation?

    He needs hope that this doesn't have to be his future. Or his kids future. Someone to speak truth into his life

4. What things would need to change if you wanted to form a relationship with those you help?

Redemptive Compassion 21

Week One: Imprisoned with Kindness

DAY TWO: Need–Focused Giving

Why do so few charitable programs attempt to holistically address the chronic need situation many people find themselves in today? Most assistance-based programs are structured around how to meet specific needs such as food, clothing, housing, and transportation, with very little attention given to the recipient of these resources. To further complicate things, many times the distribution of these resources is carried out through public venues, which can unintentionally cause humiliation or feelings of shame to the person receiving help. If one looks back in history, it was in the mid-thirties that Franklin Roosevelt's New Deal policies were instituted as an attempt to get the government more involved in helping others. Roosevelt summarized the New Deal as a "use of the authority of government as an organized form of self-help for all classes and groups and sections of our country." Initially these programs were focused on helping people provide for themselves until they got back on their feet. But through the years these programs have evolved into need-focused giving that seldom requires any participation by the recipient. Doesn't assistance that focuses on needs, not people, usually offer temporary relief that can leave the individual and their situation unchanged? Could one of the greatest challenges with need-focused giving be that while it may feed someone today, unless something changes, they'll have to be fed tomorrow also?

> **Challenge:**
> **Is it enough to meet a physical need but give little time or attention to the person in need?**

Week One: Imprisoned with Kindness

DAY TWO: Need-Focused Giving

SCRIPTURE REFERENCES

"Is it not to share your food with the hungry and to provide the poor wanderer with shelter—when you see the naked, to clothe him, and not to turn away from your own flesh and blood... and if you spend yourselves on behalf of the hungry and satisfy the needs of the oppressed, then your light will rise in the darkness, and your night will become like the noonday." —Isaiah 58:7&10

"For I was hungry and you gave me something to eat, I was thirsty and you gave me something to drink, I was a stranger and you invited me in, I needed clothes and you clothed me, I was sick and you looked after me, I was in prison and you came to visit me." —Matthew 25:35&36

"When they had finished eating, Jesus said to Simon Peter, 'Simon son of John, do you truly love me more than these?' 'Yes, Lord,' he said, 'You know that I love You.' Jesus said, 'Feed my lambs.' Again Jesus said, 'Simon son of John, do you truly love me?' He answered, 'Yes, Lord, you know that I love you.' Jesus said, 'Take care of my sheep.' " —John 21:15&16

We are clearly instructed in the Bible to meet need, but if we study Scripture it is also clear we are to focus on more than just the physical needs. In order to 'spend' ourselves on behalf of those we serve it requires us to invest holistically in their lives. It is easy to meet physical needs but much more difficult to engage, through relationship, with the person in need. Jesus instructed Peter not only to feed, but care for those he served. What changes do we need to make if we want to apply these instructions in our own life?

Week One: Imprisoned with Kindness

DAY TWO: Need-Focused Giving

CASE STUDY

Need-focused assistance was all Steve knew. His parents had routinely stood in impersonal food and assistance lines and, as an adult, he found himself modeling their lifestyle. He had little expectation that anything in his life would ever change, even though feelings of low self-esteem and shame plagued him on a daily basis. He needed the help to survive, but shouldn't something more be done to address his overall situation?

1. Why do many assistance programs appear to focus more on the need than the person in need?

   Its way easier and only requires supplies for the need. It does not do the hard work to adress the person

2. How does meeting a physical need show someone they are loved and valuable?

   You care enough to take care of them.

3. What would it take for Steve to move out of the food lines and lifestyle he had grown up in?

   Massive change. Different mindset. Help from someone who cared about him

4. Reflect on the assistance programs you are familiar with. Are they more need-focused or person-focused?

   There arnt many around

Week One: Imprisoned with Kindness

DAY THREE: Giving a Hand-Up

The greatest difference between a hand-out and a hand-up is that a hand-up requires both the giver and the recipient to share in the burden and struggle. Hand-outs offer temporary relief for legitimate needs, but can be relatively painless and struggle-free for everyone involved. All parties can remain detached and uninvolved if they choose. A hand-up requires an investment of time and resources, with combined participation by all parties for lasting change. An easy way to visualize the difference is to imagine that someone has fallen and cannot get up without help. I could give hand-outs in the form of food or a blanket and pillow, and while they would receive immediate and temporary relief, it would not help them to their feet. If I wanted to extend a hand-up, I would have to not only meet their immediate physical need, but come close enough so that I could extend my hand to them and share in their burden. As they grasped my extended hand and we pulled together it would take our combined effort and struggle for lasting results to be achieved. A hand-out is often a temporary fix to an ongoing need, but a hand-up can be life-changing for all involved.

Challenge: If giving someone a hand-up is so important why is it so seldom done?

Week One: Imprisoned with Kindness

DAY THREE: Giving a Hand-Up

SCRIPTURE REFERENCES

"But a Samaritan, as he traveled, came where the man was; and when he saw him, he took pity on him. He went to him and bandaged his wounds, pouring on oil and wine. Then he put the man on his own donkey, took him to an inn and took care of him. They next day he took out two silver coins and gave them to the innkeeper. 'Look after him,' he said, 'and when I return, I will reimburse you for any extra expense you may have.' " —Luke 10:33–35

"At mealtime Boaz said to her, 'Come over here. Have some bread and dip it in the wine vinegar.' When she sat down with the harvesters, he offered her some roasted grain. She ate all she wanted and had some left over. As she got up to glean, Boaz gave orders to his men, 'Even if she gathers among the sheaves, don't embarrass her. Rather, pull out some stalks for her from the bundles and leave them for her to pick up, and don't rebuke her.' "
—Ruth 2:14–16

Both of these stories contain examples of being offered hand-outs and a hand-up. It was important that an immediate hand-out was offered to the beaten stranger and to Ruth. But a hand-up was also needed if they were to lead full lives again. The man who had been beaten needed time for healing. The Samaritan offered not only his resources, but engaged the inn keeper as they worked together to provide ongoing assistance until the injured man was physically restored. Boaz not only offered Ruth a hand-out in the form of a meal, but also instructed his men to give her opportunities to provide for herself and her mother-in-law, Naomi. Hand-outs are often part of the hand-up process, but without an investment of ongoing time, product and participation by the recipient, they may be insufficient to bring about restoration.

⊰ Week One: Imprisoned with Kindness ⊱

DAY THREE: Giving a Hand-Up

CASE STUDY Steve had been receiving hand-outs most of his life, first as a child and then as an adult. While the food and utility assistance helped him survive, it had not and would not change his life, and required very little effort on his part. His struggle was not in getting the temporary assistance but in the emotional degradation he felt as he relied on others for daily survival. Steve needed someone willing to do more than offer immediate relief. He needed someone willing to share his burden and help him struggle to his feet.

1. Why are hand-outs so common and giving a hand-up so rare?
   Hand-outs require so little from us. Hand-ups require time, effort, and love.

2. Why are hand-outs an important component of giving a hand-up?
   We must take care of the immediate need before we can address the real issue.

3. What are some steps one could take to offer Steve a hand-up in his situation? *I think not having a steady job is a huge problem. If someone encouraged him, helped him apply, even take him to interview.*

4. What do you have to be willing to do if you want to give a hand-up and not just a hand-out?
   Be vulnerable, be honest, care enough to do something, be willing, be humble, love as Christ calls us to.

Redemptive Compassion

Week One: Imprisoned with Kindness

DAY FOUR: Charity Compassion

The most common form of compassion can be called Charity Compassion. It is a very necessary and critical component in helping people and often comes in the form of a hand-out. Charity Compassion meets genuine needs such as food, clothing and shelter. If you have ever donated to a local food or clothing drive, you have participated in Charity Compassion. Charity Compassion can be done individually and independently and often does not require an investment of much time or personal relationship. Usually both the recipient and the giver feel temporary satisfaction when it is offered. Charity Compassion is needed when addressing legitimate needs, but is usually insufficient by itself, and can create unintended negative emotions and consequences. Often the giver has the power and can appear superior to the recipient. The recipient is dependent upon the generosity of the giver and may feel inferior. This type of giving can foster a sense of inequality that further separates those who have from those who don't. Prolonged Charity Compassion can cause compassion fatigue, creating a burned-out feeling in the giver, and a left-out feeling in the recipient who must continue to rely on help from others. If Charity Compassion is not enough to produce life-transformation or change, does anyone really benefit in the long-run? The poor are stuck in poverty and the rich are stretched for adequate resources. Both feel inadequate in their roles engendering negative emotions that may be directed at each other. If Charity Compassion was enough, wouldn't it build community rather than further separate those who have resources from those who don't?

Challenge: Is meeting legitimate, immediate needs enough?

Week One: Imprisoned with Kindness

DAY FOUR: Charity Compassion

SCRIPTURE REFERENCES

"What good is it, my brothers, if a man claims to have faith but has no deeds? Can such faith save him? Suppose a brother or sister is without clothes and daily food. If one of you says to him, 'Go, I wish you well; keep warm and well fed,' but does nothing about his physical needs, what good is it? In the same way, faith by itself, if it is not accompanied by action, is dead." —James 2:14–17

"Give to the one who asks you and do not turn away from the one who wants to borrow from you." —Matthew 5:42

The Bible clearly instructs us to care for those in need. I think the challenge comes in understanding how to live out these commandments on a daily basis. I believe there is confusion in America over what constitutes a legitimate need. Often we end up feeding a want or desire that may not be critical to survival, but can cripple personal growth. If our charity becomes a lifestyle for the recipient and doesn't serve as a stepping stone to a full and productive life, does it satisfy God, or is He displeased?

Week One: Imprisoned with Kindness

DAY FOUR: Charity Compassion

CASE STUDY Steve was clearly receiving Charity Compassion on a regular basis. The food assistance met a real need of hunger, but Steve was dependent on it. How effective is any assistance program which meets basic needs but makes the recipient reliant on such support from generation to generation? Shouldn't the way we serve help others get out of need, rather than sustain them in need?

1. What do you believe God calls us to do for people in need?

    Help them, take care of the need, but also help restore them

2. Will God hold us responsible for generosity that sustains people in need, but rarely helps them move out of need?

    Yes

3. Steve was the third generation in his family to need regular assistance. What would it take to break this cycle of need for future generations?

    Change, Steve doing the hard work to break it. He would need someone to come alongside him

4. How can you live out the biblical commandment to feed and clothe the poor without creating an unhealthy dependency on further assistance?

    Give them another option. Yes feed them clothe them but also develope them. Help them to get their lives back. Give them hope.

Week One: Imprisoned with Kindness

DAY FIVE: Developmental Compassion

Developmental Compassion is not done to or for people but *with* people. It engages the giver and the recipient so both parties are an active part of the solution. It believes that everyone has something to contribute and looks for ways to empower and engage the recipient in their need. Developmental Compassion offers a hand-up, not just a hand-out, in the belief that assistance that preempts learning, self-development and growth, actually cripples and reinforces one's own helplessness in the situation. Developmental Compassion recognizes that change is a slow process and working toward lasting solutions will often be painful and difficult. This challenging process requires boundaries and clear expectations for both the giver and the recipient, as they together work toward the solution. It is usually done through community, and is strengthened by the networking and expertise a support team offers. Developmental Compassion must be married to Charity Compassion. While Charity Compassion focuses on meeting immediate needs, Developmental Compassion looks for ways to help those in need develop their full potential. One cannot provide Developmental Compassion without Charity Compassion. But should we offer Charity Compassion without incorporating Developmental Compassion in the effort?

Challenge: When we do things for people rather than with them do we hinder the development of their God given potential?

⊰ Week One: Imprisoned with Kindness ⊱

DAY FIVE: Developmental Compassion

SCRIPTURE REFERENCES

"When you reap the harvest of your land, do not reap to the very edges of your field or gather the gleanings of your harvest. Do not go over your vineyard a second time or pick up the grapes that have fallen. Leave them for the poor and the alien. I am the Lord your God." —Leviticus 19:9&10

"Joseph said to the people, 'Now that I have bought you and your land today for Pharaoh, here is seed for you so you can plant the ground. But when the crop comes in, give a fifth of it to Pharaoh. The other four-fifths you may keep as seed for the fields and as food for yourselves and your households and your children.'" —Genesis 47:20–24

Throughout Scripture we see God engaging those in need by including them in the solutions. Rather than giving instructions to pick and give food to the hungry, He said to leave some so they could pick it themselves. When famine ravaged the country people were forced to sell their land, but they received seed and permission to work the land so they could continue to provide for themselves. Finding ways to participate in providing for their need was, and still is, extremely important. Couldn't we help people flourish and reach their God-given potential better by reducing their dependency on others and helping them develop strengths within themselves?

⊰ Week One: Imprisoned with Kindness ⊱

DAY FIVE: Developmental Compassion

CASE STUDY Steve was not an active participant in his situation. He was only the recipient of what others gave and did for him. This type of charity did little to build his self-worth and self-esteem. The assistance, which was meant to help him, reinforced his belief that he did not have the capability or knowledge to be an active participant, and it played out as apathy toward life. Years of non-involvement had convinced him he was beneath those who helped him. He had resigned himself to this life of mundane existence. Convincing Steve he was capable of engaging and participating in his situation would not be done easily and would be a risky investment—not one even he was convinced was worthwhile.

1. Should one continue to help if the recipient doesn't want to participate when they can? *I think we should have patience and forgiveness however there is a point we must stop because we do not want to enable them.*

2. How would you feel if you invested in someone and in the end they still didn't change? *A little hurt however we must remember it's not about us. God is in control, and we planted a seed.*

3. What type of investment would it take to see change in Steve's life? *Both charity and developmental*

4. Which type of assistance are you more drawn to: Charity or Developmental Compassion and why?
Developmental because thats where the real change occurs.

⇥ Week One: Imprisoned with Kindness ⇤

STUDY APPLICATION: Done Individually for Group Discussion

One only has to look around at the growing need-population to see that our current helping methods are not working, and a new approach is desperately needed. Generational poverty has been growing for years and is reaching epidemic proportions. While we believe people in need can often do more to change their situation, aren't our current helping efforts also a contributing factor to the growing problem of generational poverty? Will it take all of us understanding the issues and working together if we want to see chronic need diminish in our communities? If we don't change how we help, how can we expect those we help to ever change?

> **If we don't change how we help, how can we expect those we help to ever change?**

BIBLICAL STUDY

"One who was there had been an invalid for thirty-eight years. When Jesus saw him lying there and learned that he had been in this condition for a long time, he asked him, 'Do you want to get well?' 'Sir,' the invalid replied, 'I have no one to help me into the pool when the water is stirred. While I am trying to get in, someone else goes down ahead of me.' Then Jesus said to him, 'Get up! Pick up your mat and walk.' At once the man was cured; he picked up his mat and walked…Later Jesus found him at the temple and said to him, 'See, you are well again. Stop sinning or something worse may happen to you.' The man went away and told the Jews that it was Jesus who had made him well."
—John 5:5–9, 14

Week One: Imprisoned with Kindness

STUDY APPLICATION: Done Individually for Group Discussion

1. After thirty-eight years of immobility, what was the mindset of the invalid? There was no hope of getting well

2. Why did the invalid return to the temple area where he had lived for thirty-eight years after he was healed, and why did Jesus warn him? Because that's all he knew. Jesus warned him about sin because he loved him enough to care

3. The invalid experienced a physical healing, but after thirty-eight years of begging and relying on others for all his needs he was missing some important life skills. What similarities are there between this biblical beggar and Steve's current situation? They both know there is no hope. They both are use to depending on others for survival

4. The beggar's physical body was transformed, but other transformation was necessary for him to live a full and productive life. Steve did not need a physical healing, but he did need a transformed life. What things would help transform Steve's situation and future? Relationship with Christ, people to come alongside him with some hand ups

"Our people must learn to devote themselves to doing what is good, in order that they may provide for daily necessities and not live unproductive lives."
—Titus 3:14

Referring to the above Scripture, discuss how Developmental Compassion can help someone live a productive life.

I would say the goal for Developmental Compassion is to build relationship, trust, and begin to help instill life qualities they will need to be successful. The goal is to get them back on their feet and on their own.

⊰ Week One: Imprisoned with Kindness ⊱

WEEK IN REVIEW: Individual/Group Activity

Summarize each day's key concept into a short phrase.

1. As Christians we are called to do Redeeming relationships
2. Need focused giving only addresses immediate need
3. Handups > handouts but require much more of us
4. Cherry Compassion is needed but must be paired with Dev.
5. Developmental Compassion is when we help develop people to set back on their own feet.

How have you responded (past and currently) to situations similar to what was studied this week?

Mainly Cherry sometimes serving and volunteering but not building many relationships

Based on what you're learning, evaluate what you can change or do differently when faced with similar situations in the future.

Look at people in poverty through the lenses of love and developmental compassion

What one thought, concept or statement has made the greatest impact on you this week?

Reality how government programs have failed and are actually adding to the problem.

Select one Bible verse for memorization: _____

Week One: Imprisoned with Kindness

Additional Thoughts

Additional Scriptures:
Proverbs 31:8; Romans 15:1&2; 1 Corinthians 13:3

Week One: Imprisoned with Kindness

Closing Prayer

Father God, help me develop relationships with those I seek to serve. Let me draw close enough to them so I can extend my hand and help them to their feet. Do not let me be slow to respond, but help me be wise and discerning in how I respond. Give me a heart that cares enough to work with them, not do it for them, when they can participate. Help me, Father, to do my work in such a way that it moves them closer to the abundant life you have promised each of us. May I never be satisfied only feeding them but leaving them in need. Amen.

Week Two:
The Call to Love: Is It Possible?

Week Two: The Call to Love: Is It Possible?

Case Study Story

Pastor Gary walked down from the pulpit, heading toward the crowded altar. The sermon today had been anointed and people were still slowly, tearfully, making their way forward to pray. His eyes skimmed the front and he saw many from the prayer team helping the seekers. He too felt a desire to personally engage with those at the altar. It was days like this that fueled him to stay the course. His heart was full of joy, seeing God's spirit in their midst. When he saw Sam, a new believer, he hurried toward him, anxious to join him in prayer. Just then he felt someone tug at his arm as he heard a raspy voice say "Pastor?" He turned slowly and immediately felt anxiousness seep into the joy. It was obvious the stranger came off the street. His clothes hung haphazardly, his unkempt, matted hair fell around his face. The stubble on his face was days in the making. But it was the man's eyes, staring desperately at the pastor, that pierced and unsettled Gary the most. Their red rims and muddy corneas suggested alcohol abuse. Gary looked anxiously around wondering where Bob was when he needed him most. Before his gaze could return to the man, he heard the question, the one he expected but dreaded and even more so in front of an audience. "Could you spare some money? My car's broke, I'm out of work and I'm hungry." Was it Gary's imagination or did his voice seem amplified above the other sounds? Others heard the words too and their eyes turned to their pastor to see how he would respond. His emotional high quickly descended into a sickening throb in the pit of his stomach. What would he do? What should he do? He knew money would probably not go to food or gas, but he also knew that the man wouldn't leave without being offered something. Why had this happened this morning and where was Bob, the trusted church leader, who always seemed to know what to say? The stranger moved closer, his hand out ready to announce his plea a second time. Gary reached into his pocket, his mind rationalizing his response. "God has told us to give," he thought, but he knew that his reactive response probably wouldn't really help the troubled man who stood before him. Gary struggled, confused over what to do while feelings of guilt descended like a heavy weight, crushing the joy he had felt just a few moments before. As he pushed $20 into the stranger's hand, Gary wondered—what does God want me to do?

⊰ Week Two: The Call to Love: Is It Possible? ⊱

Introduction

Church leaders, administrators and those involved in compassionate ministries are often asked for assistance from those attending the church, as well as people they don't know. Being a pastor or in a place of leadership within the church is challenging enough without also feeling unprepared for situations beyond one's control and expertise. With no plan or policy in place to help guide those responding to need requests, church leaders can struggle with what to do when asked for help. Ill-timed requests will invariably be managed by a gut reaction, not a pre-determined course of action, and often valuable resources and further ministry opportunities are lost. This week we will focus on how the church addresses need and what God's Word says about how we should respond.

> **Without a plan, ill-timed requests will invariably be managed by a gut reaction, not a pre-determined course of action.**

Week Two: The Call to Love: Is It Possible?

DAY ONE: Does Poor Planning Beget Poor Stewardship?

Churches usually agree that loving and serving their neighbors is the second greatest commandment stated in the Bible. Yet I seldom find a church that has created a plan for how they will execute and live out this command when addressing need. Requests for help are often received by a multitude of different people within the church. Without defined policies in place, how the request is addressed will depend on who hears it, how they feel about it, and what resources seem to be on hand at that moment. This often results in a knee-jerk reaction rather than a thoughtful, planned response. Lack of planning often leaves the one approached feeling pressured to do something and this can open the door to poor stewardship and a misuse and abuse of church resources. The best intentions can be misplayed without a game plan. Churches often fail in their attempt to help people in need because no one knows what to do. How can something this important be left to chance, often falling on the shoulders of one random individual who ends up representing the church through their response? Creating defined policies with a clear-cut plan allows anyone educated in the plan to respond without being influenced by a personal agenda or biased beliefs.

Challenge: Why do so few churches have defined plans or policies in place for how they will address need requests?

⚜ Week Two: The Call to Love: Is It Possible? ⚜

DAY ONE: Does Poor Planning Beget Poor Stewardship?

SCRIPTURE REFERENCES

"In Him we were also chosen, having been predestined according to the plan of Him who works out everything in conformity with the purpose of His will." —Ephesians 1:11

"The Lord Almighty has sworn, 'Surely, as I have planned, so it will be, and as I have purposed, so it will stand.'" —Isaiah 14:24

"Plans fail for lack of counsel, but with many advisers they succeed." —Proverbs 15:22

Throughout the Bible we see that God has a master plan—He believes in planning. All of creation is part of His eternal plan, nothing is randomly happening or out of control. He is not a God who rules and reacts emotionally to the requests brought to Him. He has instructed us to plan and seek wise counsel so we can have success in the things we do. Churches plan their worship services, their children and adult programs, facility needs, extra-curricular activities, and even their future growth. So why have they so seldom created plans and policies for how their church will respond and help people who come to them in need?

Week Two: The Call to Love: Is It Possible?

DAY ONE: Does Poor Planning Beget Poor Stewardship?

CASE STUDY Pastor Gary found himself in an uncomfortable, but not uncommon, situation. People within his congregation, as well as strangers, often approached him in public seeking his help. He struggled with how to respond, especially when many from his church took their own cues on how to help by watching his response. He knew his reactive responses often circumvented any further opportunity for the church to become involved. But what was he supposed to do? Having a plan in place, with trained individuals to help, would certainly allow him to respond in love, rather than haste. But no such plan existed in his church and he found himself dreading the reactive, guilt-laden responses he felt pressured to make when approached by someone requesting help.

1. Why is it important for churches to establish defined plans or policies for how they will respond to need requests?
   Without a plan then we will fail to do our job

2. How can what we feel complicate what we do when asked for help?
   Acting soley on our immediate emotions is usually a bad idea

3. Why did the audience surrounding Pastor Gary further complicate how he responded? *They were listening and watching to see what he did*

4. Does your church have helping policies in place, and if so do you know what they are? *No or I don't know about them*

Week Two: The Call to Love: Is It Possible?

DAY TWO: Imprisoned in Need

People living in generational poverty are often prisoners of their situations, in bondage and weighed down by their inability to survive without outside assistance. Too many helping entities have all too eagerly accepted the role of warden—feeding, clothing and providing shelter, but doing little to help move them out of need. Thousands of people exist in need situations, sustained by others, but they rarely experience the full life God has intended for each of us. As more and more people enter into this lifestyle, the chance of escaping diminishes. The longer they live imprisoned in need the less they can recall or relate to living differently. With each new generation that accepts this as their plight in life, the drive to live differently is diminished and will eventually be squelched. From my experience, just opening the door of their prison cell of need and beckoning them to come out is not enough. The fear of stepping out and trying it on their own is crippling. They can exist, confined within their prison of need. They aren't so sure they can survive on the outside without someone caring and providing for them.

Challenge: What has happened in our society that so many people are trapped in their situations, depending on others for basic needs?

Week Two: The Call to Love: Is It Possible?

DAY TWO: Imprisoned in Need

SCRIPTURE REFERENCES

"Is not this the kind of fasting I have chosen: to loose the chains of injustice and untie the cords of the yoke, to set the oppressed free and break every yoke?" —Isaiah 58:6

He upholds the cause of the oppressed and gives food to the hungry. The Lord sets prisoners free, the Lord gives sight to the blind, the Lord lifts up those who are bowed down, the Lord loves the righteous." —Psalm 146:7&8

"I, the Lord, have called you in righteousness; I will take hold of your hand. I will keep you and will make you to be a covenant for the people and a light for the Gentiles, to open eyes that are blind, to free captives from prison and to release from the dungeon those who sit in darkness." —Isaiah 42:6&7

God desires for everyone to live a full and prosperous life. We often mistakenly interpret prosperity through the world's lens of material success. But Scripture indicates that the life God desires for us is a life of hope and freedom, not need and oppression. People living in continual need often have no hope or plans for their future. They seldom look beyond the next week, unsure if they will be evicted, hungry or sick. Their future is unstable and unpredictable. When we so gladly feed, clothe and shelter others without encouraging them to embrace their own gifts and capabilities, do we actually help them stay imprisoned in need? What could we do differently that would free them to discover the abundant life God has called them to?

⋄ Week Two: The Call to Love: Is It Possible? ⋄

DAY TWO: Imprisoned in Need

CASE STUDY — When Pastor Gary reached into his pocket and gave the stranger $20 he did nothing to change the man's lifestyle. In fact, he probably contributed to keeping the stranger in a state of need by giving him a hand-out. From his physical appearance and demeanor, the stranger had likely been living in need for an extended period of time. His situation would not be easily addressed or turned around and would probably require some tough, as well as tender, love to make a lasting impact. This was something the Pastor was not equipped to give at that moment. What would it take to begin the process of freeing this stranger from his prison of need?

1. Are we part of God's plan to free the oppressed or have we become part of the problem? *Most places are probably the problem*

2. How have our helping efforts over the years humiliated and disgraced those we serve? *They feel inferior, and not loved or cared about*

3. Was money the right response by Pastor Gary or could there have been a better one? *No, Yes by actually sitting down with this guy and helping him*

4. What approach could you use when reaching out to someone living in generational poverty? *We must not only meet the need but also address the issue. We can give them hope in Christ that will change them.*

Week Two: The Call to Love: Is It Possible?

DAY THREE: Crippling Help

An amazingly high percentage of people living in chronic need struggle with depression. Complacency, inactivity, helplessness, and hopelessness are all contributing factors. When we do for people what they have the capability to do for themselves, we add fire to their already smoldering low self-esteem. Why do we often offer to pinch-hit for someone who is thrown a curve ball in life instead of encouraging them to stay in the game and return to bat? If we step in and do it for them aren't we making it possible for them to disengage and live life on the sidelines? Taking people out of the game usually contributes to their feelings of failure which can have a crippling, negative impact on their future. The dreams and goals we cherish most in life are often those things we struggle and work hardest to accomplish. It's not whether we fail, because we will all fail at times. It's what we do with our failures that matter. Success is usually achieved by climbing the rungs of failure on the ladder of life. When we try to cushion people from their own mistakes, because we hate to see them hurt, we often circumvent the lesson. Not letting people live through their mistakes, poor choices or failures can keep them from learning what they need to propel them on to success. It's through the trying, testing, falling and getting up experiences that we gain the strength and knowledge to live full lives. People need to be given the opportunity to live through their failures, not stay stuck in them.

Challenge: Why do so many current helping efforts seem to cripple, rather than strengthen, those being served?

Week Two: The Call to Love: Is It Possible?

DAY THREE: Crippling Help

SCRIPTURE REFERENCES

"…And we rejoice in the hope of the glory of God. Not only so, but we also rejoice in our sufferings, because we know that suffering produces perseverance; perseverance, character; and character, hope. And hope does not disappoint us, because God has poured out His love into our hearts by the Holy Spirit, whom He has given us."
—Romans 5:2–5

"You need to persevere so that when you have done the will of God, you will receive what He has promised." —Hebrews 10:36

Failing and getting back up to try again is called perseverance. Perseverance is a concept often spoken of in the Bible. Life is filled with struggles, challenges and failures, but God doesn't want us to give up and quit. He uses our difficult times to strengthen and mold us into the individuals He knows we're capable of becoming. The emerging butterfly must struggle as it breaks free from the cocoon in order to develop its wings to fly. Efforts to help free it will kill it instead. Are we crippling the very ones we want to serve by doing things for them rather than with them?

Week Two: The Call to Love: Is It Possible?

DAY THREE: Crippling Help

CASE STUDY

Pastor Gary suspected that the money he gave the stranger would not go toward what he needed, but what he wanted—another drink. Giving money that perpetuated an addictive lifestyle actually hurt rather than helped him. The stranger was crippled by his alcohol addiction and anything that aided his ability to feed this addiction was slowly killing him. Pastor Gary knew money wasn't what the man needed and that was probably why he felt sickened with guilt as he pressed the money into his dirty, shaking hand.

1. How can it cripple someone when we do something for them?

   Enabling it teaches them someone will always do something for us

2. What emotions can a person feel when they give up rather than pick up and try again?

   Failure, defeat, worthless, hopeless

3. What could the pastor have done differently that might have truly helped the man?

   Go somewhere private and talk about the alcohol addiction

4. What ways can you strengthen, not cripple, the people you help?

   By giving them a hand up not a hand out

Week Two: The Call to Love: Is It Possible?

DAY FOUR: Self-Serving or Sacrificial?

What motivates us to serve is critical in understanding why we respond the way we do. Self-serving motivation is keenly aware of and focused on how the giver feels rather than how the recipient feels or what is best for them. The giver's response is normally driven by how they'll feel if they give or how they'll feel if they don't, with the stronger emotion normally dictating the response. Sacrificial giving means we place our own emotions aside to do what is best for the recipient. Pure sacrificial giving, altruism, is rare and hard to do. Even the best attempts at serving can have hidden, self-serving agendas that fulfill something within the giver beyond what might be best for the recipient. Church groups often want to enter into service projects, but focus on how well it's going to work for them, not on where the greatest need is. They select projects by how well it fits their predetermined criteria and success is often determined by how the church participants feel once it is finished. When the motivation is more sacrificial there is less concern about the giver's agenda and more openness to serve anywhere that fills a need. A baseball player who is willing to hit a sacrifice fly so another teammate can score, must look beyond individual success and focus on what will best accomplish a win for the team. Is it possible a lot of time is wasted trying to accommodate the prerequisites of people looking to serve—time which could be better spent focused on the needs of those asking for help?

> **Challenge: What motivates us more, our own emotions surrounding our need to give, or the emotions of the person in need?**

Week Two: The Call to Love: Is It Possible?

DAY FOUR: Self-Serving or Sacrificial?

SCRIPTURE REFERENCES

"Do nothing out of selfish ambition or vain conceit, but in humility consider others better than yourselves. Each of you should look not only to your own interests, but also to the interests of others." —Philippians 2:3&4

"All a man's ways seem innocent to him, but motives are weighed by the Lord." —Proverbs 16:2

"Now it is required that those who have been given a trust must prove faithful…My conscience is clear, but that does not make me innocent. It is the Lord who judges me. Therefore judge nothing before the appointed time; wait till the Lord comes. He will bring to light what is hidden in darkness and will expose the motives of men's hearts. At that time each will receive his praise from God." —1 Corinthians 4:2, 4&5

From Scripture it appears that God looks at the motivation *behind* what we do more than He looks at what we do. We need to remember that God will expose and judge our motives and our actions at an appointed time. The enormity of these verses should cause all of us to consider what motivates us to respond to people in need. Is our motivation more self-serving or sacrificial in nature and will it ultimately please God?

Week Two: The Call to Love: Is It Possible?

DAY FOUR: Self-Serving or Sacrificial?

CASE STUDY Pastor Gary was motivated by a need to do something because of those watching him and by a hidden desire to see the man leave. His motives were self-serving which is probably why he felt so guilty about his response. Often the need to do something is driven by an emotion or desire within the giver that is seldom sacrificial. It's easy to deceive ourselves and others by an outward display of generosity, but it's impossible to deceive God. Pastor Gary knew he could have and should have done more.

1. How can one move from self-serving motivation to a more sacrificial approach? *Being aware of your motives, then also begin looking at need differently and asking, what is the best thing for the person*

2. What emotions do you experience when you appropriately withhold giving from someone who asks?

3. Do you believe Pastor Gary's motivation for giving $20 was sacrificial or self-serving?
   Self serving

4. What underlying reasons motivate you to give or withhold from others?
   I think when we give we all get that 'feel good' ① feeling. Which isn't a bad thing necessarily but it can be if that's our motivation

Week Two: The Call to Love: Is It Possible?

DAY FIVE: Does It All Come Down to Love?

The love I feel for my family is a dim reflection of the love my Heavenly Father has for me as His child. Yet there are many similarities between how I raised my children and how God has dealt with me. I taught my children essential life skills, wanting them to develop into mature and capable adults. God is constantly teaching me things that help me mature into the woman He knows I can be. My children received a lot of no's for things they wanted but didn't need or that would hurt them. God doesn't always give me what I ask for; He gives me what I need and it often comes in forms I dislike at first. When my children made poor choices or did something wrong I walked with them through the consequences of their choices, but I didn't rescue them. God also gives me free will to make my own choices and He doesn't save me when I choose inappropriately or against His will. Instead He uses my choices as opportunities to teach and mold me. So if we understand these concepts when it comes to raising our own children and we see God applying these principles to us, why do we seem so confused when it comes to helping others? Should we ask questions before we give someone what they want to make sure it's what they need? If we say no when what they want won't really help them does it mean we don't love them? Should we take more time to teach and mentor people instead of just doing things for them? Is it even appropriate to save people from the consequences of their poor choices when it might circumvent the lesson they could learn? Why don't we apply the same principles modeled by God to those we help? Is it possible it all comes down to love—we just don't love them as God has demonstrated and called us to? Could that really be the core, underlying problem?

Challenge: Is it possible to love others the same way we love our children and God loves us?

❧ Week Two: The Call to Love: Is It Possible? ❧

DAY FIVE: Does It All Come Down to Love?

SCRIPTURE REFERENCES

"*You were taught, with regard to your former way of life, to put off your old self, which is being corrupted by its deceitful desires, to be made new in the attitude of your minds; and to put on the new self, created to be like God in true righteousness and holiness.*"
—Ephesians 4:22-24

"*My son, do not make light of the Lord's discipline, and do not lose heart when He rebukes you, because the Lord disciplines those He loves, and He punishes everyone He accepts as a son. Endure hardship as discipline; God is treating you as sons. For what son is not disciplined by his father?*"
—Hebrews 12:5-7

"*For anyone who does not love his brother, whom he has seen, cannot love God, whom he has not seen. And he has given us this command: Whoever loves God must also love his brother.*" —1 John 4:20&21

We understand that God's love isn't about getting our way or having a lot of material possessions. God's love is focused on helping us mature and transform into His image. He has called us to love one another, but that doesn't mean it gives us the right to do things in His name, in love, when the end result is anything but loving. Emotions should never dictate or lead how we respond to someone's need. God's love isn't a feel-good emotion. It's caring enough to do the right thing in spite of how it feels. What does it look like when we love one another God's way?

❧ Week Two: The Call to Love: Is It Possible? ❧

DAY FIVE: Does It All Come Down to Love?

Pastor Gary was a trusted and dedicated leader of his church; he truly cared for those he served. He spent time daily discipling others in what it means to be a Christ-follower. But when the stranger came with his hand out, visibly needy, the pastor felt ill-prepared to respond. It didn't seem to be very loving to delay an immediate response for a more holistic approach. The pastor wanted to respond in love, but did he?

1. How would we respond differently to someone in need if we treated them more like our child than a stranger?

   I think we could see that they don't neccasarily know whats good for them. They know their need

2. Why does it feel so unloving to say no to what someone wants, even when it's the right thing to do?

   Maby because its so much easier to just give them what they want

3. How could Pastor Gary have shown the stranger he cared without giving him money?

   Could of tried to help with the actual issue

4. How do you respond when approached by someone in a similar situation as the stranger in this story?

   Just give them money

Week Two: The Call to Love: Is It Possible?

STUDY APPLICATION: Done Individually for Group Discussion

God calls His Church to serve people in need. But how, why, and the way we serve is critical. Understanding that a lack of planning almost always means planning for failure should motivate the church to establish policies and procedures that will guide them toward appropriate responses. It is important to understand the motives behind our actions and discern why we feel a need to respond in the way we do. We should evaluate what we hope to accomplish with respect to what we believe God would want us to do. As we strive to meet needs sacrificially, let us keep our eyes focused on pleasing God, not man, knowing we will stand before the One who looks at our heart, not at the external results of our actions.

Lack of planning almost always means planning for failure.

BIBLICAL STUDY

"One day Peter and John were going up to the temple at the time of prayer—at three in the afternoon. Now a man crippled from birth was being carried to the temple gate called Beautiful, where he was put every day to beg from those going into the temple courts. When he saw Peter and John about to enter, he asked them for money. Peter looked straight at him as did John. Then Peter said, 'Look at us!' So he gave them his attention, expecting to get something from them. Then Peter said, 'Silver or gold I do not have, but what I have I give you. In the name of Jesus Christ of Nazareth, walk.' Taking him by the right hand, he helped him up, and instantly the man's feet and ankles became strong. He jumped to his feet and began to walk. Then he went with them into the temple courts, walking and jumping, and praising God."
—Acts: 3:1–9

◁ Week Two: The Call to Love: Is It Possible? ▷

STUDY APPLICATION: Done Individually for Group Discussion

1. All his life the man had been daily carried to the temple gate, why?
   So he could beg for money
2. Who were the people who gave him alms day after day? Why didn't they do more?
   Christians, they didn't care
3. Are there similarities between how the church responded in those days and how it responds to someone in need today?
   Yes only Charitable giving
4. Peter and John did not give him alms, but they healed him through Christ's power, which transformed his life. What is required to help someone become whole and healthy?
   Jesus

"Jesus replied: 'Love the Lord your God with all your heart and with all your soul and with all your mind.' This is the first and greatest commandment. And the second is like it: 'Love your neighbor as yourself.' All the Law and the Prophets hang on these two commandments." —Matthew 22:37–40

1. What does it mean to love your neighbor as yourself?
   Well we take care of ourselves, feed, clothe, ect....
2. Do you think there are times when the Lord is displeased with how we treat people in need? Discuss why?
   Yes because we would rather just give them money then actually help them.

58 Redemptive Compassion

⁂ Week Two: The Call to Love: Is It Possible? ⁂

WEEK IN REVIEW (Indvidual/Group Activity)

Summarize each day's key concept into a short phrase.

1. Churches need to have a plan to deal with spreading
2. Need can be generational lets be apart of solution
3. We need to be careful to not enable the person
4. What are our motives for serving?
5. Do we love enough to help God's way

How have you responded (past and currently) to situations similar to what was studied this week?

I've never helped in the right way

Based on what you're learning, evaluate what you can change or do differently when faced with similar situations in the future.

Instead of giving money to a stranger tell them about Jesus who can change their life

What one thought, concept or statement has made the greatest impact on you this week? The fact that if we only have Christy compassion, or self serving motives we need to seriously look at our own lives

Select one Bible verse for memorization:_____

⚜ Week Two: The Call to Love: Is It Possible? ⚜

Additional Thoughts

_____

_____

_____

_____

_____

_____

_____

_____

_____

_____

_____

_____

Additional Scriptures:
Exodus 18:22&23; Psalm 74:21; Matthew 23:23; Acts 8:18–21; James 2:1

Week Two: The Call to Love: Is It Possible?

Closing Prayer

Father God, give me a heart that chases after Your heart when I serve my fellow man. Let it not be about me and what I need or want to do. Let me prayerfully discern, with wisdom, how You would want me to respond to someone I see in need. Convict me Father when my response is self-serving and superficially motivated by a desire to do right in the eyes of those who watch. May I be focused on pleasing You and loving others with the deep agape love You make available to me. May the things I do in Your name be pleasing to You and beneficial to those I serve. Thank you, Father God, for allowing me to be Your hands and feet to those I see in need today. Amen.

Week Three:
Seeing Through Our Father's Eyes

Week Three: Seeing Through Our Father's Eyes

Case Study Story

Laurie was pretty, but guarded, her answers short and unrevealing. She and her sister had both decided to enroll in our long-term relational program. It was her turn to be interviewed, which was a prerequisite to receiving a mentor who would assist her over the course of the coming year. Her story was familiar. She had an ex-husband who offered no support for the three children he had helped bring into the world. She was burdened with mountains of debt caused by years of emotional decisions, difficult choices, and the divorce. Her schooling had been interrupted when he left, yet she bore the degreeless debt, further accentuating her failure. Tim, her ex, had left their home and their hearts almost without notice, crushing her and the kids with his indifference. His new girlfriend consumed all his time and money, making sure Tim didn't pay child support or see the kids, both of which Laurie desperately needed. Beaten and emotionally dry, she poured herself into her children. Their lives had been turned upside down and she felt responsible even though she couldn't control Tim's actions. She spent money she didn't have trying to buy them happiness. While Laurie's story was far too common, what was different was the magnitude of smoldering anger she kept in check. Questions would cause it to surface, but she'd quickly squelch it. I could tell she just wanted to get through the interview and leave. As I finished my questions I asked if I could pray for her again, not knowing that question would cause an eruption of pent-up emotions. She burst into tears, yelling at me, "Pray? Why pray to a God that allows things like this to happen? If there is a God why did He let Tim hurt me and my children by leaving and ignoring us? How could a loving God do that to any child?" Oh, I could pray alright, she said, but she hated God with every ounce of her strength. He had done this to her. He could have prevented Tim from leaving. He could have made Tim love his children even if he didn't love her. She was done with God. She wanted nothing to do with a God who would do what He had done. Her outburst quieted to a dejected sob with tears flowing and hands clenched. I quietly asked her if she really felt God had done this to her and her children? Biting her lip, she wiped her eyes and whispered, "If there really is a God, why doesn't He love me and my children. What did we do to deserve this?"

Week Three: Seeing Through Our Father's Eyes

Introduction

When times are hard it can be really difficult to believe that God cares for us or even sees us. Many of the people I talk to feel abandoned and ignored by God. They feel guilty because of the choices they've made, and believe they are unworthy of anyone's love, much less God's. Some, like Laurie, blame their situation on God and struggle to manage their anger at a Being they can't see. Often our understanding of God is based on our circumstances and relationships. For one living in a crisis of need, that image can be very negative and unloving. One of the most critical components in helping people move out of need is to help them see their worth and value to God. Once they start to understand their Creator, they start to understand themselves. This week is all about seeing people through our Father's eyes.

> **A critical component in helping people move out of need is to help them see their worth and value to God.**

Week Three: Seeing Through Our Father's Eyes

DAY ONE: God's Value System

One of the most critical components in helping people is to first see them through God's eyes. Most of what the world esteems as valuable is in direct contrast to what God values. Success, money, good looks, skills, degrees, status, power, who we know, or who knows us, are all considered important in today's society. But God's rating system doesn't work that way. In fact, most of the people highlighted throughout the Bible would have been termed failures, non-achievers, unimportant, weak, inadequate, dangerous, and useless in our modern culture. At a service I attended the speaker shared three points that changed how I approach people in need. He challenged us to see people through God's eyes, to see their value and worth to the God who created them, before we attempt to serve them. He suggested that until we see them as valuable to God we will not value them appropriately as we work with them. Once we understand their value we become willing to invest in them—and invest we must if we really want to impact their lives. He closed with this thought—our investment will produce dividends as they in turn invest in others, returning full circle God's gift of redemption. Three simple points—see their value, invest in them, and receive a return on the investment. And then it dawned on me, isn't that exactly what Jesus always did?

Challenge: Would we respnd to people differently if we could see them through God's eyes?

Week Three: Seeing Through Our Father's Eyes

DAY ONE: God's Value System

SCRIPTURE REFERENCES

" 'But Lord,' Gideon asked, 'how can I save Israel? My clan is the weakest in Manasseh, and I am the least in my family.' " —Judges 6:15

"When Jesus reached the spot, He looked up and said to him, 'Zacchaeus, come down immediately. I must stay at your house today.' So he came down at once and welcomed him gladly. All the people saw this and began to mutter, 'He has gone to be the guest of a sinner.' " —Luke 19:5–7

"As Jesus was walking beside the Sea of Galilee, He saw two brothers, Simon called Peter and his brother Andrew. They were casting a net into the lake, for they were fishermen. 'Come, follow me,' Jesus said, 'and I will make you fishers of men.' " —Matthew 5:18&19

The Bible is full of examples of people on the fringe—the weak, those caught in sin, and the marginalized—the very ones Christ spoke to and God recognized. The disciples were common fishermen who were not chosen to be mentored by church leaders. Yet Jesus looked beyond their earthly credentials and saw men worthy of His investment. That investment continues to reap benefits and rewards 2,000 years later. Is it possible, with Christ's help, to see beyond who someone appears to be, into the potential that lies within them?

Week Three: Seeing Through Our Father's Eyes

DAY ONE: God's Value System

CASE STUDY Laurie had been devalued by her husband and she felt unworthy of God's love. She needed someone to speak eternal value into her life, breaking the chains of hate that bound her. Laurie didn't need things, she needed a new perspective of herself. She believed she was unlovable and her guarded and difficult behavior confirmed to herself that she was impossible to love. One of the best ways to help Laurie was to invest relationally in her life. We couldn't just tell her how much God loved her, we needed to show her.

1. How can one see beyond the person and situation and into the potential buried treasure inside?

    By looking through the lenses of grace

2. What ways can negative emotions affect the way we behave?

    Sometimes we make a base judgement about someone and immediately decrease their value

3. How could love be spoken into Laurie's life that wouldn't seem demeaning or fake? *Tell her about God's love, His grace, and that there is a chance to start over. Her value is based on more than just what she has done.*

4. Why would acknowledging someone's value to God make us more inclined to invest in them relationally?

    We understand His love for them, how He sees them.

Week Three: Seeing Through Our Father's Eyes

DAY TWO: One Common Thread

Over the years I have met with many individuals and couples who were enrolled in our programs, interviewing them to match them with a volunteer mentor who would help them achieve their goals. While each story is different, there is a common thread that weaves its way through them all. This thread seems to influence everything about the enrollee's current situation and grows stronger the longer they stay in need. It seems to be woven into their DNA and dictates how they see themselves and others. It controls their reactions and responses to life. All of us are prone to this influence and many of us are silent carriers. Unaware of what we are doing, we cripple the very ones we desperately want to help. So what is this thing that permeates everything about each person I interview? What common denominator seems to influence and control them? People in chronic need carry a negative self-image in their minds and feel inferior to those around them. Anyone who experiences need for any extended period begins to see themselves and their world in a negative light. It's as if life's challenges and personal failures destroy their self-worth rather than serve as stepping stones toward understanding and success. How we respond to their need has the power to confirm or reverse this crippling and infectious mental image. If someone feels embarrassed and humiliated, do we build them up when we make them stand in public lines to receive help? If we do things for people when they have the potential to do it for themselves, are we reinforcing their belief that they are incompetent and helpless? Doesn't focusing on the need, rather than the person, contribute to their feelings of being unlovable and worthless? Do you think there have been times when you might have inadvertently hurt the very ones you've tried to help?

> **Challenge: What common, destructive thread are we weaving recklessly through the tapestry of so many lives?**

Week Three: Seeing Through Our Father's Eyes

DAY TWO: One Common Thread

SCRIPTURE REFERENCES

"Then Caleb silenced the people before Moses and said, 'We should go up and take possession of the land, for we can certainly do it.' But the men who had gone up with him said, 'We can't attack those people; they are stronger than we are.' And they spread among the Israelites a bad report about the land they had explored. They said, 'The land we explored devours those living in it. All the people we saw there are of great size…Joshua son of Nun and Caleb son of Jephunneh, who were among those who had explored the land, tore their clothes and said to the entire Israelite assembly, 'The land we passed through and explored is exceedingly good. If the Lord is pleased with us, He will lead us into that land, a land flowing with milk and honey, and will give it to us.' " —Numbers 13:30–32, 14:6–8

"Do not let any unwholesome talk come out of your mouths, but only what is helpful for building others up according to their needs, that it may benefit those who listen." —Ephesians 4:29

The Israelite community had wandered in the desert for years, and many had lost confidence that their lives were ever going to change. They no longer believed in God's promises and resigned themselves to a difficult, mundane existence, unable to see things in a positive light. They chose to listen to the lies and negative report of the majority and missed out on the fertile land God had prepared for them. When people are discouraged and struggling they are prone to see everything from a negative perspective. Could the things we say or do prevent people from embracing the life God has planned for them? Does our talk or actions build them up, according to their needs, or does it tear them down according to their fears?

Week Three: Seeing Through Our Father's Eyes

DAY TWO: One Common Thread

Laurie had an extremely negative image of herself. She felt like a failure. From her perspective, she had failed in her marriage, failed in her education, failed as a provider for her family, and failed as a parent because she couldn't control her ex-husband's lack of interest in their children. This negative self-image permeated everything about her life and merely giving her stuff was never going to restore her self-worth. She needed more than stuff—she needed a new mental image of herself if she was going to heal and become whole.

1. What are some common ways we address need that could be tearing someone down rather than building them up?

    By not speaking truth into their broken mindset

2. When we give reactively, what negative emotions and poor self-image do we tend to reinforce?

    That people feel bad for them because they are less, hopeless

3. What things could be done to help build Laurie's low self-esteem?

    Speak truth into her life then help her see that for herself

4. If you believe you may have contributed to someone's poor self-image through your giving response, what can you do differently next time?

    by having developmental compassion

Week Three: Seeing Through Our Father's Eyes

DAY THREE: The Art of Listening

Has listening become a lost art? In our fast-paced society it seems almost counter-cultural to slow down and listen before we respond. Most of us are used to getting what we want, going where we want, doing what we want, when we want and we're put off by anything that slows us down. But if we're going to focus on the person, and not just their expressed need, we're going to have to slow the process down and listen. Sadly, those asking for help probably won't embrace a slower response. The truth is it's going to take a lot more energy on everyone's part, both the giver and the recipient, to hear the story before a response is made. But it is in listening that we gain insight and understanding needed to truly help someone. It's in the listening that a relationship begins. Listening is hard and requires patience on the part of the listener. Being quick to solve problems implies the recipients are incapable, inadequate and ignorant about their own situation. But we need to listen to more than just the person requesting help before we respond. biblically we are told to seek and listen to wise counsel from others when making decisions. But the most significant and important thing we can do is go to God in prayer before we do anything else. God is involved in every life. He allows us opportunities to help others, but we are not His only resource. It takes time to listen for God's promptings before we begin responding. If we don't take time to listen to the person in need, seek and listen to counsel from others and listen for God's still, small voice, how will we know how to respond?

> **Challenge: Why do we seldom take the time to really listen to those we want to help?**

Redemptive Compassion 71

Week Three: Seeing Through Our Father's Eyes

DAY THREE: The Art of Listening

SCRIPTURE REFERENCES

"The proverbs of Solomon son of David, king of Israel: for attaining wisdom and discipline; for understanding words of insight; for acquiring a disciplined and prudent life, doing what is right and just and fair; for giving prudence to the simple, knowledge and discretion to the young—let the wise listen and add to their learning, and let the discerning get guidance—for understanding proverbs and parables, the sayings and riddles of the wise. The fear of the Lord is the beginning of knowledge, but fools despise wisdom and discipline." —Proverbs 1:1–7

"He who answers before listening—that is his folly and his shame." —Proverbs 18:13

"Why spend money on what is not bread, and your labor on what does not satisfy? Listen, listen to me, and eat what is good, and your soul will delight in the richest of fare. Give ear and come to me, hear me, that your soul may live. I will make an everlasting covenant with you, my unfailing kindnesses promised to David." —Isaiah:55:2&3

"My dear brothers, take note of this: everyone should be quick to listen, slow to speak and slow to become angry." —James 1:19

I was told there are 322 verses related to listening in the Bible—God thinks it's important. He constantly counsels us to listen to Him. He knows that unless we take the time, we cannot enter into the life-changing relationship He desires to have with us. One of the ways we show value and worth to people is giving them our time, and listening takes time. Attentive listening communicates worth. If we can't take time to hear their story, what does that really communicate to them?

Week Three: Seeing Through Our Father's Eyes

DAY THREE: The Art of Listening

CASE STUDY During my interview with Laurie, she answered all my questions. As I listened, however, I realized there was a lot she wasn't saying that I needed to hear. My decision to pray with her a second time after the interview is when God opened the door to her heart so I could understand the depth of her struggle. If I had been in a hurry I would have missed what was really going on and our helping efforts would have been complicated by deeper, unexpressed needs. I find that once people understand you really care about them they will open up to you. I had earned the beginning of Laurie's trust and it was the first step on a long journey to wholeness.

1. Why is it so hard to listen before we respond?
   Sometimes the solution can seem obvious to us, however we are not in their shoes

2. What vulnerability is there on the listener's part if they take the time to hear someone's story?
   I think it requires vulnerability on both sides. The person who has to open up and the other must be willing to go into that.

3. If Laurie hadn't opened up, how might our response to her need been different?
   We wouldn't be addressing the core issue

4. Are you a better communicator or listener and why are both important?
   Listener
   We must listen to begin to understand that person and their struggles. Then God may give us an opportunity to speak truth and life into that

Week Three: Seeing Through Our Father's Eyes

DAY FOUR: Reflecting the Image of Our Creator

Is it possible to truly understand ourselves if we don't know the one who created us? We are complicated beings and the image we carry of ourselves has been influenced by many different factors, including our past, our relationships, and our successes and failures. But does our past or present have to define what our future can be? Too often our perceptions are based on an earthly standard and not viewed from a heavenly perspective. People trapped in need seldom have a positive image of themselves. The person they see in the mirror is often someone who has failed, is beyond redemption, defeated, unloved, unworthy, or an array of other negative labels. Because they don't see their potential, they set the bar low and live lives beneath their capacity and capabilities. We have an amazing opportunity to help them see themselves mirrored in the image of Christ, reflecting their hidden potential buried deep inside. It's important to affirm their personal worth to God, and that He intimately knows and cares for them. One of the most powerful tools we have is the ability to speak words of affirmation to those we help. We can begin by helping them understand they have been uniquely, not randomly, created in His image. We can encourage them to draw on His strength when they feel weak, and empower them through His promises for their future, giving them hope. We can reflect their potential in Christ until they begin to believe it themselves. Words are one of the most powerful tools at our disposal, but without care they can become weapons of destruction rather than be used for life transformation. What do your words say to others about your Creator?

Challenge: How much does the perception we have of ourselves affect how we behave?

Week Three: Seeing Through Our Father's Eyes

DAY FOUR: Reflecting the Image of Our Creator

SCRIPTURE REFERENCES

"So God created man in His own image, in the image of God He created Him; male and female He created them." —Genesis 1:27

"For you created my inmost being; you knit me together in my mother's womb. I praise you because I am fearfully and wonderfully made; your works are wonderful, I know that full well. My frame was not hidden from You when I was made in the secret place. When I was woven together in the depths of the earth, your eyes saw my unformed body. All the days ordained for me were written in your book before one of them came to be."
—Psalm 139:14–16

" 'For I know the plans I have for you,' declares the Lord, 'plans to prosper you and not to harm you, plans to give you hope and a future.' " —Jeremiah 29:11

Using Scripture to affirm value, worth, and uniqueness is powerful. God knows us intimately and what He sees when He lovingly looks at us is not who we presently are, but who we've been created to be. Speaking worth to each other, using God's own words, is a resource we always have at our disposal. The power that is released when His Word is spoken to others is beyond our ability to understand. Try to envision yourself from God's perspective—what does His Word say about how He sees you?

Week Three: Seeing Through Our Father's Eyes

DAY FOUR: Reflecting the Image of Our Creator

CASE STUDY — Whenever I have opportunity I try to speak affirming words to those I am with. As I prayed for Laurie, I spoke of God's great love for her, her worth to Him, and the hope I saw for a bright future. I could see her demeanor change just through the spoken word, even though it would take time for her to believe. There is power in the spoken word, especially when it is God's Word. If we only focus on the need, will we miss the opportunity to be used as an instrument of God to speak hope and worth to another?

1. Why do so many in need have a poor mental image of themselves?

2. When we feel unworthy and unloved, how does it affect our behavior?

3. Why do you think Laurie's demeanor changed when I prayed with her after her emotional outburst?

4. Do you believe you must do some physical act of service for someone before you have really helped them?

Week Three: Seeing Through Our Father's Eyes

DAY FIVE: Daring to Dream Again

People who live in chronic need often lose their ability to hope, dream and make plans for their future. Life becomes a matter of survival and their daily existence often feels almost unbearable. As people withdraw from living, the life within them seems to dry up. Decisions are made for the moment. Choices are impulsive based on how they feel, with little consideration of how a decision made today will affect tomorrow. Living a full life is replaced with a mundane existence of complacency and resignation.

Challenge: When people lose hope, do they quit trying to improve their situation and enter survival mode?

Restoring hope and helping people dream and reach their goals are important in redeeming people from lives of chronic need. When I interview people I ask them what they would like to see changed or accomplished in six months, one year and beyond. Most have difficulty answering these questions because they haven't thought about their future for a long time. Helping them remember their passions and dreams can start them on a life-changing journey. A critical component for someone who hasn't dared to dream for a while is to help them set achievable goals that, when accomplished, will serve as stepping stones toward a new and brighter future. As these small seeds of hope take root and start to grow, they begin to understand that a different life is within their grasp if they are willing to work toward it. If a life without hope has no meaning or purpose, could restoring hope be the greatest gift we can give someone?

Week Three: Seeing Through Our Father's Eyes

DAY FIVE: Daring to Dream Again

SCRIPTURE REFERENCES

"Let us hold unswervingly to the hope we profess, for He who promised is faithful. And let us consider how we may spur one another on toward love and good deeds." —Hebrews 10:23&24

"As they talked and discussed these things with each other, Jesus himself came up and walked along with them; but they were kept from recognizing Him. He asked them, 'What are you discussing together as you walk along?' They stood still, their faces downcast. One of them, named Cleopas, asked Him, 'Are you the only one living in Jerusalem who doesn't know the things that have happened there in these days? ... But we had hoped that he was the one who was going to redeem Israel.'" —Luke 24:15–18, 21

"May the God of hope fill you with all joy and peace as you trust in Him, so that you may overflow with hope by the power of the Holy Spirit."
—Romans 15:13

When Jesus was crucified, the disciples were crushed. They had placed all their hope in Him and now their dreams were gone. They found themselves downcast, discouraged, and hopeless. But Jesus reminded them never to lose hope because God is faithful and the Author of all hope. As a Christ-follower we can remind those who are struggling that there is hope. What would happen if we did what Jesus did and walked beside those who have lost hope? Could it potentially change the world?

Week Three: Seeing Through Our Father's Eyes

DAY FIVE: Daring to Dream Again

CASE STUDY

Laurie was hopeless and angry when I first interviewed her. She felt stripped of her future and trapped in her circumstances. She was suffering from more than the loss of her husband. She had lost the life they were building together, the stability she had felt, and the plans they had laid for their future. But most of all, she had lost hope. Her dreams and plans had been smashed to pieces and it felt as if there was nothing more to look forward to. She needed someone who would encourage her to dream new dreams and help her set and achieve goals that would move her toward a future filled with hope.

1. Why do you think someone trapped in need might give up and quit trying?

2. When hope is lost, what other areas in one's life are affected?

3. What goals might Laurie set that could help her find hope in her future?

4. How can you help restore hope to someone going through a difficult time?

Week Three: Seeing Through Our Father's Eyes

STUDY APPLICATION: Done Individually for Group Discussion

The most important thing to remember when we're about our Father's business is that it is His business, not ours. It requires us to conduct ourselves in such a way that we promote and represent Him honorably. The saying that we may be the only Bible people read is true. Many people will draw their opinions of God based on what they see and hear us do in His name. We have an amazing opportunity to see others as God does, to speak of His value and love for them, and to point them in His direction. *"Therefore, my dear brothers, stand firm. Let nothing move you. Always give yourselves fully to the work of the Lord, because you know that your labor in the Lord is not in vain."* —1 Corinthians 15:58

We may be the only Bible people read

BIBLICAL STUDY

"When a Samaritan woman came to draw water, Jesus said to her, 'Will you give me a drink?' (His disciples had gone into the town to buy food.) The Samaritan woman said to Him, 'You are a Jew and I am a Samaritan woman. How can you ask me for a drink?' (For Jews do not associate with Samaritans.) …The woman said to Him, 'Sir, give me this water so that I won't get thirsty and have to keep coming here to draw water.' He told her, 'Go, call your husband and come back.' 'I have no husband,' she replied. Jesus said to her, 'You are right when you say you have no husband. The fact is, you have had five husbands, and the man you now have is not your husband. What you have just said is quite true.' …Then, leaving her water jar, the woman went back to the town and said to the people, 'Come, see a man who told me everything I ever did. Could this be the Christ?'…Many of the Samaritans from that town believed in Him because of the woman's testimony, 'He told me everything I ever did.' So when the Samaritans came to Him, they urged him to stay with them, and He stayed two days. And because of His words many more became believers." —John 4:7–9, 15–18, 28&29, 39–41

⁂ Week Three: Seeing Through Our Father's Eyes ⁂

STUDY APPLICATION: Done Individually for Group Discussion

1. Why is the Samaritan woman such an unlikely candidate for Jesus to use in His evangelistic work?

2. What do you think Jesus saw in her, when others just saw a sinful woman?

3. What negative emotions might the Samaritan woman and Laurie have shared due to their life choices and circumstances?

4. Imagine a conversation between Laurie and Jesus. What might Jesus say to her?

5. Do you think the Samaritan woman's personal encounter with Jesus changed her life? How could Laurie's life change if she renewed her relationship with Christ?

Many came to know Christ because of the Samaritan woman's testimony. Why do you think Jesus chose to work through her? What testimony might Laurie have if she became a believer in Christ?

Week Three: Seeing Through Our Father's Eyes

WEEK IN REVIEW (Indvidual/Group Activity)

Summarize each day's key concept into a short phrase.

1. _____

2. _____

3. _____

4. _____

5. _____

How have you responded (past and currently) to situations similar to what was studied this week?

Based on what you're learning, evaluate what you can change or do differently when faced with similar situations in the future.

What one thought, concept or statement has made the greatest impact on you this week?

Select one Bible verse for memorization:_____

Week Three: Seeing Through Our Father's Eyes

Additional Thoughts

Additional Scriptures:
Psalm 31:24, 33:18, 42:5, 100:3, 119:130, 139:17&18, Proverbs 12:18, 15:22, 16:24, 23:18; Isaiah 64:8; Jeremiah 31:3, Lamentations 3:22&23; Luke 12:7; 2 Corinthians 1:3&4, Philippians 4:19; 1Thessalonians 5:11

Week Three: Seeing Through Our Father's Eyes

Closing Prayer

Father God, help me see others through Your eyes. Help me look beyond who they are and see the potential that lies within. Give me a heart to invest in them because they have great value to You. Help me understand how my responses can hurt them more than help them. Use me as a restoration tool in their life. Give me ears to listen and a heart to discern. May I always seek wise counsel from You and those around me who know You. May I understand the power of my words so I can speak affirmation and encouragement into their lives. Use me as a conduit to restore hope and help others dream again. I pray most of all that because they know me, they will come to know more of You. Amen.

Week Four:
Tough Love for Tough Times

⚜ Week Four: Tough Love for Tough Times ⚜

Case Study Story

Randy and Kathy sat quietly in my office, looking anywhere but at each other. I sensed brokenness in Randy and aggression in Kathy. I could tell before a word was spoken she was only here to make a point. Whatever had happened behind closed doors had shut her down emotionally. As I prayed before we began, I asked for strength and wisdom to get to the bottom of what was going on. They answered the questions politely, both speaking when spoken to, but nothing more. Then I asked, "Why are you here? What do you want from Love INC?" Kathy responded quickly, wanting to say her piece first, her story tumbling out dramatically. She had wanted this program months ago, hoping it would save the marriage, but Randy wouldn't come. Their marriage had continued to crumble and she finally kicked him out of the home. She was done, it was over. His drinking was out of control and she wanted nothing more to do with him. "And then," she said with disgust, "Randy did the most bizarre thing." She went on to explain that he had started coming to the program by himself, the very program he had refused to attend when she still had hope. It had enraged her, as if now it would make any difference. She only agreed to come to the interview because she wanted to make sure her side was heard. They weren't divorced yet and their money was still tangled together. She didn't want him making decisions about money without her. "All this is his fault. He's the one with problems and he has destroyed our lives," she said as she delivered her final blow. Then it was Randy's turn and as I turned to him, the sadness in his eyes was raw and extreme. He agreed he hadn't wanted to come before. He had a drinking problem and he had pushed her to the edge. But he was ready to do whatever it would take to save his marriage and keep his family intact. His voice trembled as his eyes begged me to offer them something to grab hold of. "Do you work with couples who are not even living together?" he quietly asked. I sat for a moment, contemplating the months that would lie before them. It wouldn't be an easy path and would require difficult choices, hard work and forgiveness between them. I looked at Kathy whose deep hurt was camouflaged in aggression and anger. I had once been where she was and I had given up. I knew Kathy didn't have any idea

⊰ Week Four: Tough Love for Tough Times ⊱

Case Study Story

how difficult divorce would be, but I did, and I believed it was worth fighting to keep their marriage together. My answer was complicated, laying out requirements and restrictions that would challenge them both. But I hoped their story could be different from mine and I was willing to take a chance. Ultimately it would be up to them. Would they be willing to take the tough steps required to turn their situation around?

Week Four: Tough Love for Tough Times

Introduction

Change is hard. We all know it. We're creatures of habit and once the habit is formed it's really hard to change. Helping people climb out of difficult situations, and deep places of need, requires a lot of work and commitment on everyone's part. But can we really make lasting changes without God's help? I've found we can take positive steps toward a different life, but true, lasting transformation requires God's involvement. Working toward a new way of thinking and living takes a lot of hard work. The journey to a new life is best done with a community of others who offer encouragement and accountability as they celebrate each step with you. This week we'll take a look at some of the tough steps required for change, and how it takes a body of believers working together to accomplish God's redeeming work of transformation in others.

Lasting transformation requires God's involvement.

Week Four: Tough Love for Tough Times

DAY ONE: The Domino Effect

When I used to think of someone in need, I had the preconceived notion that they needed money or the things money could buy. Through the years I have learned that need is directly linked to the lack or loss of important resources that are needed to live full and abundant lives. Physical, financial, relational, emotional, mental, and spiritual resources are essential and build on each other. The more resources a person has, the easier it is to build other ones. But the opposite scenario is also true. When resources diminish a domino effect occurs, increasing need with each one that is diminished. If someone becomes sick and loses their physical health, the first resource is affected. Because they are sick they can't work so they become financially strapped and another resource is diminished. The lack of money causes them to lose their home which puts strain on their marriage and the relationship resource is in jeopardy. The emotional and mental strain causes depression, affecting their mental and emotional resources. As the depression deepens they lose faith that God cares and the spiritual resource is weakened. As each of these resources diminish or disappear, the need situation grows. Someone who has lost a number of important resources will seldom be able to work their way out of need on their own. Most people in need have an accumulation of deficient resources yet we respond by meeting immediate needs such as food, paying one month's rent, or other obvious things. The process of building up depleted resources cannot be accomplished by merely giving money or stuff, it requires much more. Since resources build on each other, how does one begin the process of holistically addressing the overall situation?

Challenge: Does one have to be financially poor to be in need?

Week Four: Tough Love for Tough Times

DAY ONE: The Domino Effect

SCRIPTURE REFERENCE

"But Naomi said, 'Return home, my daughters. Why would you come with me? Am I going to have any more sons, who could become your husbands? Return home, my daughters; I am too old to have another husband. Even if I thought there was still hope for me—even if I had a husband tonight and then gave birth to sons—would you wait until they grew up? Would you remain unmarried for them? No, my daughters. It is more bitter for me than for you, because the Lord's hand has gone out against me!'" —Ruth 1:11–13

Naomi had suffered great loss in her life. Almost all of her resources had disappeared and she felt hopeless and full of despair. But God had other plans for her and eventually her resources were rebuilt and she had a full and complete life again. Most people in need are like Naomi, with a multitude of different factors intertwined that affect the situation. We often feel need is directly linked to the lack of money or stuff. But if we ignore the physical, relational, emotional, mental, and spiritual health of the person, our helping efforts will be inadequate and ineffective overall. Is it possible to have very little money but live a full and resourceful life?

❧ Week Four: Tough Love for Tough Times ❧

DAY ONE: The Domino Effect

CASE STUDY Randy and Kathy were not financially poor, but the domino effect in their life had depleted almost every resource. Their finances were a mess, the marriage was broken, relationships were fractured, health was compromised by stress and alcohol, leaving them emotionally dry and mentally on the edge. Their faith was almost non-existent as they tried to hide from their church and God the shame they felt. There wasn't any "thing" we could give them that would address their overall situation. But with God's help, and the body of Christ surrounding them, they had a good chance of achieving wholeness and fullness in their lives once again.

1. Why is it almost impossible to achieve or affect lasting change without addressing the full range of resources in one's life?

   If we only address the surface issues how are we going to help with the deeper real issues?

2. How can we live full and abundant lives with very little money?

   Contentment with Christ

3. Can you identify some of the resources Randy and Kathy needed restored in their lives? *relational, emotional, mental, spiritual*

4. Which resources do you believe are the most important in your life and why?

   Spiritual, emotional, mental. As long as I am walking with God I know I'll be okay. I have to keep my emotions in line, so that I have a clear head mentally.

Week Four: Tough Love for Tough Times

DAY TWO: Collective Spiritual Discernment

Do we respond to someone's need as if God is intimately involved in their life? Wouldn't acknowledging that He knows, cares and is able, remove the burden of the situation from us as individuals? That doesn't mean we don't have work to do. It means we collectively, through prayer, and with other believers, discern the different roles in problem-solving: God's, ours and theirs. Everyone has a part to play. God calls us to be radically generous and lovingly discerning, but we must be careful not to undermine the order He has established. Compassion and justice are both critical—God did not intend or equip us to do or be everything for everyone. How often do we try to play all the parts as if we're the only player on the team? God doesn't choose to play our part or their part and we would be unwise to attempt His part or the recipient's part. Prayerfully using collective spiritual discernment will help us determine the right response in every situation. Let's imagine the need is either a boulder or a backpack. Boulders represent the heavy stuff that cannot be carried alone and needs our help. Backpacks represent the things that can be carried without help. Carrying backpacks for others because they are weak, struggling or lazy will only further weaken them in the long run. Wouldn't it be more beneficial for those we help if we moved them towards independence not increased dependency? Coming together in prayer as a body of believers, seeking spiritual wisdom and discernment, can become a powerful conduit through which God can flow His redeeming power. Could it be that often we have been playing God instead of praying to God when responding to need?

Challenge: Is it important to pray and wait before responding to someone's need?

Week Four: Tough Love for Tough Times

DAY TWO: Collective Spiritual Discernment

SCRIPTURE REFERENCES

"So the Twelve gathered all the disciples together and said, 'It would not be right for us to neglect the ministry of the word of God in order to wait on tables. Brothers, choose seven men from among you who are known to be full of the Spirit and wisdom. We will turn this responsibility over to them and will give our attention to prayer and the ministry of the word.'" —Acts 6:2–4

"There are different kinds of gifts, but the same Spirit. There are different kinds of service, but the same Lord. There are different kinds of working, but the same God works all of them in all men." —1 Corinthians 12:4–6

"Instead, speaking the truth in love, we will in all things grow up into Him who is the Head, that is, Christ. From Him the whole body, joined and held together by every supporting ligament, grows and builds itself up in love, as each part does its work." —Ephesians 4:15&16

God's Church is the body of believers coming together for the common purpose of discerning His will, doing His work, and bringing Him glory. For the body to be complete, each part must understand and perform its individual role. As the body of believers grew in the early days of Christianity, the disciples struggled to keep everyone fed and cared for. They recognized they couldn't do it all and wisely appointed others, gifted in the area of benevolence, to administer the task. Too often we respond to need as if we alone make up the body. We try to do things that limit involvement from others who could also help. Christ is the head. If we cut off the head, how effectively can the body function?

⊰ Week Four: Tough Love for Tough Times ⊱

DAY TWO: Collective Spiritual Discernment

As I listened to Randy and Kathy's story I knew it was going to take a community of believers, committed to using collective spiritual discernment, to restore their lives. The needs were huge, far beyond the ability of just a few to meet. It was critical we understood what God was doing, what He wanted us to do, as well as what He knew Randy and Kathy must do to get healthy. Understanding our roles and working as a community of believers is where our strength would lie. Their family's future was hanging by a thread, and we needed to make sure our actions didn't become the noose that strangled them to death.

1. What are some of the reasons collective spiritual discernment isn't being practiced more when helping others?

   1) We don't seek God about it
   2) We want the credit
   3) We want to be in control

2. What emotions might we struggle with as we seek to discern the different roles and only do our part?

   Pride, jealousy, envy, frustration

3. What are some of the roles Randy and Kathy need to play to help heal their situation?

   Kathy will have to learn forgiveness and see the effort to change by her husband. Also realize we all have problems

4. What damage might be done if you carry someone's backpack for them when they could carry it themselves?

   Enablers

Week Four: Tough Love for Tough Times

DAY THREE: Speaking the Truth in Love

Do you think it is common for people to manipulate others to get what they want? Twisting facts, telling lies and hiding information are all common ploys for people in desperate situations. If questioned or confronted about their need, they will often display emotions such as anger, with threats and tears, to hopefully intimidate the giver into getting what they want. Confronting inappropriate behavior or responses is hard and if done incorrectly or with selfish motives is wrong. But does God want us to blindly turn the other cheek when we suspect dishonest or destructive behavior? When we make the choice not to confront don't we join them in living the lie? We are often willing to speak truth to someone we know and love, but act as if it's not loving to speak truth to someone we don't know who is requesting help. Doesn't speaking truth in love really communicate we care enough to not accept the lie and that we expect honesty and truth in our relationship? Perhaps taking the time required to get to the truth communicates we are willing to do the hard stuff because they're worth it. I've heard people say "I don't ask questions when helping others because it's really not my business or place to ask." But when someone involves you by asking for help in their situation, doesn't it become your business? Have you ever thought about what really happens inside the individual who displays this type of manipulative behavior and wins? Do you think they feel victorious that they got their way or devalued because the time and energy required to work through to truth wasn't given?

Challenge: Why do we seldom ask questions, even when we think someone isn't being totally honest?

Week Four: Tough Love for Tough Times

DAY THREE: Speaking the Truth in Love

SCRIPTURE REFERENCES

"Have nothing to do with the fruitless deeds of darkness, but rather expose them." —Ephesians 5:11

"For the time will come when men will not put up with sound doctrine. Instead, to suit their own desires, they will gather around them a great number of teachers to say what their itching ears want to hear. They will turn their ears away from the truth and turn aside to myths." —2 Timothy 4:3&4

"He who rebukes a man will in the end gain more favor than he who has a flattering tongue." —Proverbs 28:23

"Then we will no longer be infants, tossed back and forth by the waves, and blown here and there by every wind of teaching and by the cunning and craftiness of men in their deceitful scheming. Instead, speaking the truth in love, we will in all things grow up into Him who is the Head, that is, Christ." —Ephesians 4:14&15

"But if the watchman sees the sword coming and does not blow the trumpet to warn the people and the sword comes and takes the life of one of them, that man will be taken away because of his sin, but I will hold the watchman accountable for his blood." —Ezekiel 33:6

Why do we often behave as if it is not Christ-like to seek truth? Jesus was uncomfortably honest and confrontational when He needed to be. He did not ignore deception, but always exposed it, even looking into the hearts of those around Him. The Bible is filled with teachings and warnings about dishonest, selfish gain. If we allow others to continue in destructive, harmful lifestyles, without attempting to change their course through truthful confrontation, will we also face consequences from God? Could it be easier to confront the liar than to be confronted by God if we don't?

Week Four: Tough Love for Tough Times

DAY THREE: Speaking the Truth in Love

CASE STUDY

Randy and Kathy were used to manipulating each other, and had been living lives of deception for a long time. Randy drank to escape the realities in his life that he couldn't change. Kathy, unable to control his drinking, spent money they didn't have to get back at him. She didn't recognize that her excessive shopping sprees contributed to and were a big part of the problem. They had deceived each other to the point that truth was obscured and difficult to recognize. Before their situation could start to heal there had to be a lot of truth spoken in love. Those first months of exposing the lies and deception would be very painful and difficult. But once the lies were exposed, they could start rebuilding a relationship based on honesty and trust.

1. Why is it so difficult to confront or ask questions when someone asks for help? *1) It almost seems insulting or makes us look unloving*

2. Confrontation never feels loving when you're in the middle of it, why is that? *I'm not sure it's hard*

3. Why was it critical to get to the truth before Randy and Kathy's relationship could start to heal? *To get everything back in the open. Start with clean slates*

4. What things can you do that will help you speak the truth in love? *Understand its more loving than just being nice. Need to develope more boldness, courage*

Redemptive Compassion 97

Week Four: Tough Love for Tough Times

DAY FOUR: Choices and Consequences

Life is filled with choices and all choices have consequences but is it important for people to experience the consequences of poor choices? In my community, landlords are extremely tolerant with negligent renters, only to have the delinquent renter cry out to others to save them from impending homelessness when faced with eviction once their non-payments catch up with them. Many families receiving food stamps will spend them frivolously in the first part of the month, relying on local food banks to bail them out at the end of the month when they run short. And tax refunds are seldom applied to past debt, but often squandered in unnecessary purchases, propagating the unending cycle of bankruptcy as a viable option for uncontrolled spending. The way we meet need often allows those who have made a poor choice to continue to make those same choices as we bail them out of their circumstances. Learning comes from living through poor choices, not from being saved from them. When the lesson is circumvented, the need to make a better or different choice in the future is not learned. Sadly we have helped create a culture of people who don't have to make a good choice because almost always someone will help them when their poor choice becomes a crisis. Being held accountable for our choices and experiencing discipline by living through the consequences means we will learn how to heed correction and learn from our mistakes. Is our desire to help alleviate pain in reality crippling people from becoming healthy and whole? Do we help people lean into their future by allowing them to learn from their past or do we sabotage their future because we try to save them from their past? Why should someone's crisis of the moment, which was years in the making, receive an emergency response?

Challenge: Is it unloving to allow someone to live through the consequences of their choices?

Week Four: Tough Love for Tough Times

DAY FOUR: Choices and Consequences

SCRIPTURE REFERENCES

"He who ignores discipline despises himself, but whoever heeds correction gains understanding." Proverbs 15:32

"No discipline seems pleasant at the time, but painful. Later on, however, it produces a harvest of righteousness and peace for those who have been trained by it. Therefore, strengthen your feeble arms and weak knees. 'Make level paths for your feet,' so that the lame may not be disabled, but rather healed." —Hebrews 12:11–13

"Do not be deceived: God cannot be mocked. A man reaps what he sows." —Galatians 6:7

God allows us to make choices and decisions about how we will live our life and while He has given us the right to choose, He has also made it very clear that there will be consequences for our choices. Throughout the Bible we see people making poor choices and then living through extreme and even deadly consequences. God doesn't save us from, or bail us out of, the painful situations we create. He uses them as opportunities to teach and mold us as we move through life. So if God believes consequences are an important tool for shaping people, shouldn't we also?

Week Four: Tough Love for Tough Times

DAY FOUR: Choices and Consequences

CASE STUDY Randy and Kathy needed to make some new and better choices if we were going to work with them as a couple. Randy was already feeling the consequence of his unresolved drinking problem. Going to a substance-abuse program for healing was a choice he had to make to participate in our program. Kathy had to make some difficult choices in her relationship with Randy, including forgiveness and a willingness to try again. Through the months ahead they each would face decisions that would be pivotal for their family. Their future together did not have to be dictated by their past. They could have a transformed life together if they wanted to—the choice was up to them.

1. What do we teach someone when we save them from a self-imposed crisis? *That someone is always going to save them. That their actions don't have consequences*

2. Why is it difficult to watch someone live through the consequence of a poor choice they've made? *Because we want to take control and help alleviate the pain*

3. As Randy and Kathy made some difficult choices, how could the support of others help them succeed? *To encourage them to not give up.*

4. What are some ways you could help someone that would not circumvent the opportunity for them to learn?
   *1) let them learn
   2) Pass along wisdom / warnings
   3) Help them see why they are where they are*

Week Four: Tough Love for Tough Times

DAY FIVE: But I Need It!

We live in a 'if I want it, then I deserve it and I'll find a way to get it' culture. What we really need has become unrecognizable in a world of instant gratification. Much of the poverty and need experienced today has been brought on, or is complicated by, the mentality that because I want it, I need it. People enrolled in our programs struggle distinguishing between wants and needs. The more affluent our American society has become, the more removed we are from what our real, basic needs are. The actual things needed to survive are very minimal. A lot of what is currently asked for and given charitably in America addresses wants, not needs, and almost never pertains to a real life or death situation. What happens to people when we focus on what they want and ignore the greater, underlying needs that should be addressed? Does anything change long-term or do we just enable an unhealthy day-by-day existence? We are a materialistic society and giving people the stuff they want makes everyone feel better for a moment. But are we giving people what they want at the expense of what they need, because we're unwilling to make the sacrifice required to meet their real need? To effectively address poverty, we may need to change how we respond. Perhaps the core problem really is a need versus want dilemma—it's not just that the things people *want* they often don't *need*. It's also that what they most *need* is not something we *want* to do or give. Could it be that meeting real needs is just too much of a sacrifice on everyone's part?

Challenge: Why is it so difficult to tell the difference between what we want and what we need?

❧ Week Four: Tough Love for Tough Times ❦

DAY FIVE: But I Need It!

SCRIPTURE REFERENCES

"So do not worry, saying, 'What shall we eat?' or 'What shall we drink?' or 'What shall we wear?' For the pagans run after all these things, and your heavenly Father knows that you need them." —Matthew 6: 31&32

"A man's life does not consist in the abundance of his possessions." —Luke 12:15

"And my God will meet all your needs according to His glorious riches in Christ Jesus." —Philippians 4:19

"The woman said to the serpent, 'We may eat fruit from the trees in the garden, but God did say, 'You must not eat fruit from the tree that is in the middle of the garden, and you must not touch it, or you will die.' 'You will not surely die,' the serpent said to the woman, 'For God knows that when you eat of it your eyes will be opened, and you will be like God, knowing good and evil.' " —Genesis 3:2-5

From the beginning of time there has been confusion over what we want versus what we need. Even in the Garden of Eden, Eve was tempted by something she wanted, not something she needed and it caused the fall of mankind. The substance of our lives should not revolve around the stuff we've accumulated but it often does. God has promised to meet our needs. Why is it so hard to believe that He will take care of us?

≈ Week Four: Tough Love for Tough Times ≈

DAY FIVE: But I Need It!

CASE STUDY Randy and Kathy came with a long list of what they wanted, but most of it wasn't what was really needed to save their marriage and transform their home. They had spent the last few years trying to run from their problems with alcohol and emotional shopping sprees, both of which just further complicated their situation. What they most needed only God could give them and as they submitted their own agendas to Him, He started to heal them from the inside out and true transformation took hold.

1. Why is it often easier to give people what they want than press deeper into what they need? *takes less effort on our part*

2. Why is it so hard for us to identify what we need versus what we want? *Our society tells us we deserve it*

3. Why was it important for Randy and Kathy to become submissive to God for true healing to occur? *Both had to humble themselves, forgive themselves*

4. How should you respond when what someone wants isn't what they really need? *with the truth in a loving way*

⁂ Week Four: Tough Love for Tough Times ⁂

STUDY APPLICATION: Done Individually for Group Discussion

This week we have studied just how difficult it can be to meet needs holistically. So often we treat symptoms that do nothing to build the resources desperately needed in our lives. A surface need almost always means there are deeper, undisclosed needs. It is critical that we collaborate as a community of believers to collectively, spiritually discern what God is doing, what He is calling us to do, and what He wants the individual in need to do. As we begin the task of addressing the deeper needs, we will have to speak honestly and communicate the difficult, tough choices ahead for all involved. It will take great strength and fortitude to allow the consequences of choices to run their course, no matter how painfully unloving it appears at the time. Doing what is needed is almost never what we want to do. But if we're going to be about our Father's work, isn't it what we're called to do?

> **Doing what is needed is almost never what we want to do.**

BIBLICAL STUDY

"Now Naaman was commander of the army of the king of Aram. He was a great man in the sight of his master and highly regarded, because through him the Lord had given victory to Aram. He was a valiant soldier, but he had leprosy… So Naaman went with his horses and chariots and stopped at the door of Elisha's house. Elisha sent a messenger to say to him, 'Go, wash yourself seven times in the Jordan, and your flesh will be restored and you will be cleansed.' But Naaman went away angry and said, 'I thought that he would surely come out to me and stand and call on the name of the Lord his God, wave his hand over the spot and cure me of my leprosy. Are not Abana and Pharpar, the rivers of Damascus, better than any of the waters of Israel? Couldn't I wash in them and be cleansed?' So he turned and went off in a rage. Naaman's servants went to him and said, 'My father, if the prophet had told you to do some great thing, would you not have done it? How much more then, when he tells you, "Wash and be cleansed"?' So he went down and dipped himself in the Jordan seven times, as the man of God had told him and his flesh was restored and became clean like that of a young boy." —2 Kings 5:1, 9–14

☙ Week Four: Tough Love for Tough Times ❧

STUDY APPLICATION: Done Individually for Group Discussion

1. Naaman was a respected and powerful man, but he lived with great need in his life. Because of his leprosy what other resources in his life were affected? *physical*

2. Naaman was put off by Elisha's response in several ways. Why did Elisha respond the way he did and why did it make Naaman so angry? *It made Naaman angry because he had to do something*

3. What emotions do you think the servants felt when they approached and challenged Naaman to make a different choice? What consequences would Naaman have experienced if he ignored the offered help because it wasn't what he wanted? *Probably scared of how he would react / wouldn't of gotten healed*

4. Imagine some of the tough love conversations that had to take place with Randy and Kathy to begin the restoration process. Discuss what choices they had in front of them and what the possible consequences would be of their choices. *Divorce, giving up, or forgiveness restoration*

5. Both Naaman and Randy and Kathy had a lot to gain and a lot to lose, depending upon what they chose to do. Talk about the similarities between these two stories.

Naaman had a disease, when he went to go get help he was looking for a handout not requiring much of himself. He even turned angry that he had to act to get help. However with the encouragement of people speaking truth into their life he did. Randy also had a problem and was looking for help. However Kathy did not seem supportive of it anymore. Through the process she had to humble herself and they both had to do the hard work to get it done.

⚜ Week Four: Tough Love for Tough Times ⚜

WEEK IN REVIEW (Indvidual/Group Activity)

Summarize each day's key concept into a short phrase.

1. When one resource drops it tends to affect the others
2. Importance of relying on God for wisdom in responding
3. If we truely love people we will tell them the truth
4. We must allow people to live through their choices sometimes
5. Discern the difference between peoples wants and needs

How have you responded (past and currently) to situations similar to what was studied this week?
Probably been an enabler. Didn't look into the persons story or situation.

Based on what you're learning, evaluate what you can change or do differently when faced with similar situations in the future.
1) Give only what people need
2) love enough to speak truth
3) Don't rescue people from their choices

What one thought, concept or statement has made the greatest impact on you this week?
"learning comes from living through poor choices not being saved from them

Select one Bible verse for memorization:_____

⇥ Week Four: Tough Love for Tough Times ⇤

Additional Thoughts

Additional Scriptures:
Zechariah 8:16&17; Philippians 4:19; Colossians 3:9&10, 4:4–6; 1 Corinthians 12:12&18; 2 Corinthians 6:3&7

⊰ Week Four: Tough Love for Tough Times ⊱

Closing Prayer

Father God, holistically helping others is impossible without You. Help me never to respond casually to need requests I might hear. Would I always come before you to understand what You are doing and what You want me to do. Help me to understand my role in the Body of Christ and don't let me think I'm more important than I am. Would I not be afraid to lovingly speak the truth and bring Your light into dark situations. Help me not to circumvent the lessons and cripple the wounded by saving someone from the consequences of their choices. Give me the strength to not give into what they want because I don't want to take the time to address what they need. May I always strive to be a vessel You can use for redeeming the broken, helping restore them to the fullness of life You have promised us. Amen.

Week Five: Healing from the Inside Out

# Week Five: Healing from the Inside Out …

Case Study Story

The older couple sat before me, emotionally distraught and physically agitated. It had been more than an hour of conversation, the interview process digging deeply into Robert and Sarah's personal lives. It was their second marriage and the adult children were from her past not his. I sensed that most of what I said Robert agreed with, if not audibly, at least internally. Sarah wiped tears from her eyes and clutched at Robert's hand, wanting him to back her up and be on her side. How could she make Jeff, her adult son, move out of their house again? They had tried so many times before, but she always let him back in, especially when he had nowhere else to go. She was scared, but I watched Robert pull back his hand, stifling his frustration. This conversation wasn't new to them, but had always been their secret until now. They could get in trouble. Jeff was out on parole for drug use, back to his ways and hiding in their home. If we were going to help them the first step would involve moving Jeff out, who was complicating their own chance of getting a hold of their life. But Jeff had control of Sarah and she couldn't seem to break it. He had probably manipulated her most of his life, learning early how to get his way. But childhood tantrums had escalated into lifestyle behaviors that were threatening not only him, but them. Jeff had told her he would kill himself if she made him leave again and she believed him. I tried to explain that even though he blamed her, she wasn't responsible for his actions. He was an adult and would do what he wanted, but it seemed impossible for her to grasp any truth in my words. Robert's voice escaped before he could stop it spilling his own fear that Jeff might die in their home if they didn't do something. Through tears and trembling he said he didn't know if he could stick around until that happened. I heard Sarah moan and watched her wince, as she secretly sensed the truth in his words. To further complicate things, they were raising her daughter's son, Charlie, who at the tender age of five already controlled them with his tantrums. Even getting to this interview had been challenging. It was canceled twice because he was out of control. Both of her adult children had bounced in and out of their home and jail, struggling with addictions, divorce, joblessness, and debt. As much as it was tearing Sarah

⊰ Week Five: Healing from the Inside Out ⊱

Case Study Story

apart, she needed to be needed by them—it was what defined her. Had they come to us too late? Had this lifestyle of need, poor choices, and co-dependency stolen their ability to believe it could be different? My mind narrowed in on the little boy caught in the middle. Unless something changed, Charlie's future would probably follow a path similar to his mother or Uncle Jeff. As I waited for their answer, I prayed silently that God would give both them and me the strength to do the right thing.

⇥ Week Five: Healing from the Inside Out ⇤

Introduction

Is the strength or weakness of a nation directly related to the strength or weakness of the family units within that nation? Have positive role models and mentors disappeared in many children's lives and do they grow up without experiencing the discipline, structure and work ethic necessary for them to lead productive lives? Each family trapped in generational poverty has the high probability of passing that same lifestyle on to their children unless something changes. Often those who have relied on assistance from others for generations are difficult to engage in programs that require change and participation from them. Their dependency on others to provide for them seems to have absolved them of feeling any personal responsibility for their own welfare. The problems are multi-faceted, deeply entrenched, and a learned lifestyle that will not be easily addressed or changed. If the number of American families in crisis is reaching epidemic proportions, what will it take to turn it around? This week we will look behind closed doors at the pervasive moral erosion, compromised values, and lack of positive role models that characterizes so many homes.

> **Each family trapped in generational poverty has the high probability of passing that same lifestyle on to their children.**

Week Five: Healing from the Inside Out

DAY ONE: About Our Father's Business

When I first started doing ministry work I thought I would feel good most of the time about what I was doing. But the harsh reality surfaced almost immediately as I daily fought through challenges, disappointments, ridicule and criticism. I quickly learned that being about my Father's business wasn't going to be easy and shouldn't be something I engaged in casually. Don't we often think that if we're in God's will everything will fall into place and that struggles indicate we have taken a side road or veered off course? But perhaps the truth is that easy or hard doesn't really indicate anything. We are told we cannot understand things from God's perspective so why are we surprised when it's hard or the end results are different than we expected? I have learned I must be willing to do what He asks and leave the results in His hands, even though it may leave me confused, disappointed, or even humiliated or humbled once it's finished. On many occasions we

Challenge: Why is it so difficult to know if one is working within God's will?

will have to choose who we are trying to please—man or God. God's ways are not the way of the world and well-intentioned suggestions can actually divert us from the task we've been called to. Those watching from the sidelines won't always understand or agree with the choices and decisions you'll feel led to make. But it isn't about giving people what they want, or saying what they want to hear or even trying to please the crowd. It's about discerning what God wants you to do and then persevering through to the end. It takes clear vision and singleness of purpose not to let applause or ridicule, fame or obscurity, success or failure deter us from the work He's given us to complete. But how can we know if it's His work if we don't ask Him? Could it be that if we don't pray before we work we might do a good work, but not necessarily His work?

Week Five: Healing from the Inside Out

DAY ONE: About Our Father's Business

SCRIPTURE REFERENCES

"Whatever you do, work at it with all your heart, as working for the Lord, not for men, since you know that you will receive an inheritance from the Lord as a reward. It is the Lord Christ you are serving." —Colossians 4:23&24

"Therefore, my dear brothers, stand firm. Let nothing move you. Always give yourselves fully to the work of the Lord, because you know that your labor in the Lord is not in vain." —1 Corinthians 15:58

"Am I now trying to win the approval of men, or of God? Or am I trying to please men? If I were still trying to please men, I would not be a servant of Christ." —Galatians 1:10

Throughout the Bible there are many instructions on how to work for the Father but it also seems apparent that His work is often hard and we must guard against getting distracted, weary or off-course. Jesus was not confused or distracted about what He came to earth to do and neither was Paul, who when faced with trying to please both man and God, knew he must choose God. Carrying our cross will not be easy, but is it supposed to be? How can we find the strength to persevere and end strong when we're struggling and those around us are suggesting we quit?

Week Five: Healing from the Inside Out

DAY ONE: About Our Father's Business

CASE STUDY Robert and Sarah's interview was one of the hardest I've ever done. As Sarah collapsed sobbing on the floor, convinced forcing Jeff to leave would cause him to kill himself, I internally questioned myself. My head could make sense of all the issues, but my heart wanted to give in and let Jeff stay. I knew the deep-seated problems in their home revolved around the dysfunctional relationships in the family and giving in wouldn't help them. I had to let them make the choice—quit and continue in their downward spiral, or take the first of many difficult steps toward change.

1. Why does God sometimes involve us in things that from all human standards seem sure to fail?

   To humble us, to test us, build character and perseverance

2. If we can't use emotions to gauge if something is in line with God's will, what should we use?

   Prayer, seek God asking Him for wisdom

3. Why was it so important that Jeff move out of the house?

   1) So he can't control his mom 2) He is destroying new marriage 3) They could potentially go to jail

4. Explain why you believe applause can or cannot distract as much as ridicule.

   I think ridicule is worse because it makes you question what God has said. Applause sounds like your doing it right but we must be careful not to fall into pride.

Week Five: Healing from the Inside Out

DAY TWO: Engaging Those We Serve

Do you believe that anyone who has the capacity and capability to participate in their need situation should do so, no matter how limited that capacity might be? How does one convince someone they can be part of the solution when they can get what they want without participating? For generations, many have received assistance with minimal or no involvement on their part and it can feel almost criminal to insist they do something—but is it? What does God want? Do you believe that He wants those in need, not just those who serve them, to become actively involved in the solutions to their needs? If things are going to change, won't both the giver and the recipient have to be willing to do things differently? But change is difficult, uncomfortable, and slow and most of us don't choose change until our other options run out.

Challenge: What should we do when those asking for help won't do their part?

So how do we encourage people to take a chance on themselves and become involved in finding solutions for their situation? How do we convince them to participate when they have other choices that don't require them to? Is it important for helping entities to agree that involving the recipient is important so we work together and not against each another? Understanding how to engage the people we serve is complex and not easily answered, but I believe we must persevere in understanding what God would want us to do in each situation. Helping efforts that stifle rather than develop one's capabilities can be crippling. Do we really want people to become whole and healthy or are we satisfied that they remain dependent on us?

Week Five: Healing from the Inside Out

DAY TWO: Engaging Those We Serve

SCRIPTURE REFERENCES

"And we urge you brothers, warn those who are idle, encourage the timid, help the weak, be patient with everyone."
—1 Thessalonians 5:14

"All Scripture is God-breathed and is useful for teaching, rebuking, correcting and training in righteousness, so that the man of God may be thoroughly equipped for every good work." —2 Timothy 3:16&17

"And the Lord's servant must not quarrel; instead, he must be kind to everyone, able to teach, not resentful. Those who oppose him he must gently instruct, in the hope that God will grant them repentance leading them to a knowledge of the truth, and that they will come to their senses and escape from the trap of the devil, who has taken them captive to do his will."
—2 Timothy 2:24–26

These scriptures provide us with guidance on how we should engage with others. We are to warn or rebuke those caught in self-destructive or lazy lifestyles. But we are also called to encourage and help those who are weak. We are called to correct and train people—to mentor them through loving relationships as they learn. We are told to be patient and give them time, which means we're willing to invest our time as long as they also stay invested in the effort. Everyone has potential—we just have to learn how to tap into it and together seek knowledge, accept conviction, apply correction, and practice, practice, practice until it gives birth to new life.

⇥ Week Five: Healing from the Inside Out ⇤

DAY TWO: Engaging Those We Serve

CASE STUDY Robert and Sarah were deeply trapped in generational poverty. Their lifestyle had always been supplemented by help from others without their own personal involvement. The change needed was substantial and would require their full participation. They knew something had to change, but did they understand that they had to change? Their decision to stay or leave the program would be life-changing, for better or for worse. Was it too much too late, or was there still hope?

1. Why is it important for helping entities to work together when trying to meet need? *Because the recipient will go wherever has the least amount of effort put in.*

2. How important is encouragement when someone is trying to do things differently? *Extremely, we have to understand some of these people have been trapped in poverty for generations. Its extremely hard to change.*

3. Why did Robert and Sarah feel very little personal responsibility for their situation? *Robert - because it wasn't his sin*

4. If you decided to teach, mentor and encourage someone, what would you have to be willing to do? *Be vulnerable, honest, kind, gracious, patient, loving*

Week Five: Healing from the Inside Out

DAY THREE: I Must Do Something

Which is more important, that we do something, or that we do the right thing when helping someone? I have often heard people say, "I don't care if someone takes advantage of what I give them. My responsibility is to give what I can without question or judgment and leave the rest up to God." When I first started working in ministry I too struggled with what my Christian responsibility was when approached by someone in need. Then I had a dream. I was standing before my Lord and Savior and He said to me, "Lois, you have done a lot of things in my name through Love in the Name of Christ." Then I was shown two answers, one of which I know I will hear one day. The first was the answer I want, "Well done my good and faithful servant." But the second answer changed my response to need from that day forward. He said, "I wasn't involved in those things you did in My name. Why didn't you ask Me what I was doing and what I wanted you to do?" I realized that from that point on doing the right thing was more important than just doing something. Could it be that how, why and what we do is as important, if not more important, than if we do anything at all? Sympathy, the ability to enter into, understand, or share someone else's feelings, is usually reactive, impulsive, and emotionally driven by the need to do something. Empathy, on the other hand, is the ability to identify with and understand someone else's feelings or difficulties, but to engage the head as well as the heart. It is more thoughtful, slower in response, and driven by the desire to do the right thing, not just anything. What happens when our sympathetic giving enables or even encourages people to continue living dishonest or destructive lifestyles? Will God hold us equally accountable for *how* we respond, not just *if* we respond?

> **Challenge: Is it better to do at least something for someone than nothing at all?**

Week Five: Healing from the Inside Out

DAY THREE: I Must Do Something

SCRIPTURE REFERENCES

"To do what is right and just is more acceptable to the Lord than sacrifice."
—Proverbs 21:3

"He has showed you, O man, what is good. And what does the Lord require of you? To act justly and to love mercy and to walk humbly with your God."
—Micah 6:8

"It is not good to have zeal without knowledge, nor to be hasty and miss the way." —Proverbs 19:2

We are called to show mercy and justice, but don't we often lean heavily on the mercy side, forgetting the commands to also act justly? Why is it so hard to do both when we help people in need? Perhaps the underlying problem is driven by our desire to respond quickly. There are many Scriptures warning us that haste is not pleasing to God and that He wants us to prayerfully seek His will before we act. Could it be that praying is the real work in any ministry and the effectiveness of our work will be directly tied to the frequency and sincerity of our prayers?

⊰ Week Five: Healing from the Inside Out ⊱

DAY THREE: I Must Do Something

CASE STUDY There were so many needs in Robert and Sarah's life. They were almost paralyzed in their ability to do anything, and the temptation to step in and do something for them was extremely strong. Neither of them was working, their health was poor, all their relationships seemed fractured and dysfunctional, plus their financial situation was in total chaos. There was substance abuse, parole violations, and the grandchild who was being pulled in multiple directions and disciplined by no one. With so much need, wouldn't doing anything be better than doing nothing?

1. How can one show both justice and mercy to someone in need?

   Tell them the truth but in a loving gracious way.

2. What emotions will you feel if you slow your response down when someone asks for help?

   Calm, at peace before you respond

3. If Robert and Sarah choose to leave the program, should we still try to engage with them on a lesser level?

   I would say yes try and continue to engage however tell them if they want help they must commit first

4. Do you usually pray before you act, or do you often act first and then hope God will bless it?

   Depends on situation but regardless I need to seek God first all the time.

Week Five: Healing from the Inside Out

DAY FOUR: Raising Up a Child

Reflecting back to your childhood, who had the greatest influence on your life? Many of us can think of people who impacted and helped shape us as we grew. But wasn't it our parents and the environment we grew up in that influenced us the most? I know from years of helping families there is a significant need for strong parenting skills and positive role models within the home. But there is also a great need for the adults within the home to understand and accept their personal responsibility to provide for their own family whenever possible. This disengagement by the adults within the home to raise and provide for their own children is weakening the family unit and eroding the stability and strength of our nation. Have we unintentionally contributed to this problem by responding to children's needs as if they were orphans? We often provide children with essential resources such as food and clothing without attempting to teach, mentor or help the parent provide for their own family's needs. The more we engage without teaching, the more disengaged the parent or adult can become, which can hurt the child's future and can further perpetuate this lifestyle into the next generation. Parents who are not parenting or providing for their own families complicate their children's chances of learning the concepts and skills necessary for them to lead a productive life as adults. With the absence of effective parenting in many homes, children grow up without experiencing discipline, boundaries, expectations and consequences. As these children grow into adults, they find themselves unable to successfully navigate in a world they can't control or manipulate. Perhaps the best way to change the future of the next generation is to work with the parents of this generation.

Challenge: How much influence can we have on a child's future if we don't change the environment they're being raised in?

Week Five: Healing from the Inside Out

DAY FOUR: Raising Up a Child

SCRIPTURE REFERENCES

"Discipline your son, for in that there is hope; do not be a willing party to his death." —Proverbs 19:18

"He who heeds discipline shows the way to life, but whoever ignores correction leads others astray." —Proverbs 10:17

"If anyone does not provide for his relatives, and especially for his immediate family, he has denied the faith and is worse than an unbeliever." —1 Timothy 5:8

"Endure hardship as discipline; God is treating you as sons. For what son is not disciplined by his father?" —Hebrews 12:7

The Bible is filled with instruction for parents. Discipline is important and the job of parenting is not one to be taken lightly. Many of the verses in Proverbs not only give instruction but also contain a warning of what will happen if it is ignored. God is our Heavenly Father and He disciplines us as His children so we can live a full and productive life of righteousness and peace. If we focused on strengthening the families we help rather than absolving them of personal responsibility, wouldn't we also strengthen our communities and ultimately our nation for generations to come?

Week Five: Healing from the Inside Out

DAY FOUR: Raising Up a Child

CASE STUDY

Sarah had struggled raising her children as a single parent before she married Robert. She felt unloved as a child and in her attempt to show love to her own children, proceeded to raise them in an environment without discipline, boundaries, or consequences. The result was that the adult children used manipulation to control others, negatively affecting all areas of their lives. Charlie was being raised in the same volatile environment and was learning the same coping skills he witnessed from the adults around him. Unless the home environment changed, or a strong, very involved adult became part of his life, Charlie was destined to follow the poor example of his parents and grandparents.

1. What problems in our society might be traced back to a lack of good parenting, or positive role models in a child's life?

   1) Fatherless homes 3) No work ethic
   2) No respect for authority

2. What things from your childhood had a major impact in shaping who you are today?

   1) Work ethic from dad 3) Mom instilling God in me
   2) Learning how to save 4) The outdoors

3. Why do you think Sarah was controlled by her children and even by Charlie, her grandson?

   Partly she felt unloved as a child so she wants to be loved by her kids so she lets them run wild

4. How would you go about helping someone learn new parenting skills?

   Teach them about the importance of discipline. How much of an impact the parents have on their children

☙ Week Five: Healing from the Inside Out ❧

DAY FIVE: Fruit from Our Labor

Christians are often drawn to acts of service as a form of evangelism. When the person they are helping doesn't show outward signs of Christian growth, does it mean they have failed? I hadn't been working for Love INC very long before I found myself struggling to answer those who wanted to know if the people we helped were accepting Christ and showing up at churches. We were helping a lot of people but what was our eternal impact? I know we cannot assume that people in physical need don't know Christ, as often they have a very close, personal relationship with Him. But what about those who don't know Christ, do they see Him in us? Are they drawn to know more of Him because of our service to them? Is there a spiritual harvest as a result of our planting? Then one night I had a dream that gave me the confidence to believe we don't need to know the end result.

Challenge: In ministry, why do we often feel we must bring people to Christ to have successfully served them?

In my dream I realized that knowing and harvesting aren't necessarily part of the job—it's up to God to decide what part we play. Our job is to be obedient and do whatever He asks, whether it is to plant seeds, water, fertilize, pull weeds, tend the field, or reap the harvest. I have personally found that I seldom get to see the fruit of my labor, which has served to keep me humble and reliant on Him. I have had to learn not to gauge success based on what I can see. The farmer who sows seed cannot keep digging the seed back up because he can't see it growing—he will destroy his crop. Instead he must do each task with great care and wait patiently for the seed to sprout, take growth, and mature. Perhaps we need to spend less time concerned about what we can see and more time trusting that God can work through our efforts if we commit each step to Him. What does it take to continue in faithful service even when we can't see the fruit from our labor? What does God think of workers who need guaranteed results to stay the course?

Week Five: Healing from the Inside Out

DAY FIVE: Fruit from Our Labor

SCRIPTURE REFERENCES

"So neither he who plants nor he who waters is anything, but only God, who makes things grow. The man who plants and the man who waters have one purpose, and each will be rewarded according to his own labor. For we are God's fellow workers; you are God's field, God's building." —1 Corinthians 3:7–9

"Even now the reaper draws his wages, even now he harvests the crop for eternal life, so that the sower and the reaper may be glad together. Thus the saying 'One sows and another reaps' is true. I sent you to reap what you have not worked for. Others have done the hard work, and you have reaped the benefits of their labor." —John 4:36–38

We are called to be Christ's hands and feet and we must be dedicated and faithful in the role He has given us. We make up the body of Christ and each part is significant in its own way. How we work may be more important than what we do. Perhaps the most important thing we can do is to work in such a way that if someone doesn't know Christ, they'll want to know more about Him because of what they see in us. Can we expect to bring a person to Christ if we don't have time to be Christ to them first? Someday we may get to see the beautiful bouquet God created from our efforts. But do we have enough faith to do our part, even if we never get to pick a flower?

Week Five: Healing from the Inside Out

DAY FIVE: Fruit from Our Labor

CASE STUDY Robert and Sarah left our program prematurely, the commitment more than they were willing to give. Seeds were sown, but they couldn't endure the weeding process required to see good growth, so they ran. Did we fail? I know we tried to be Christ through our actions and we often shared His great love for them with our words. I don't know where they are today, but God does. During the time they were with us, we did our part as well as we could and I believe that's all God expects.

1. How can we serve people and share Christ without assuming or implying they do not already know Christ?
   1) know them by their fruits
   2) ask them

2. When we get to see the end results of our work why do we often have a greater sense of accomplishment?
   We get to see the positive impact we have had

3. Should we have compromised what was expected to keep Robert and Sarah from quitting? No

4. In your opinion what elements need to happen to successfully serve someone?
   1) To love on em!
   2) To be humble
   3) Be willing

Week Five: Healing from the Inside Out

STUDY APPLICATION: (Done Individually for Group Discussion)

What goes on in the home behind closed doors is shaping the future of our country. If we want to strengthen our nation don't we have to strengthen the families who make up the nation? Often the people who try to take steps to better their situation are penalized through the loss of benefits and support they would continue to receive if they did nothing. The magnitude of children who have been labeled with behavioral or learning disabilities is staggering. Are these children being encouraged to underachieve because their parents cannot afford the loss of the disability income if their child improved? Disregarding the future by sustaining people in need with little thought to how it is affecting the next generation should concern us. Do you believe the Church can do more to help with this national crisis?

Sustaining people in need with little thought to how it is affecting the next generation should concern us.

BIBLICAL STUDY

"*The word of the Lord came to Jonah son of Amittai: 'Go to the great city of Nineveh and preach against it, because its wickedness has come up before me.' But Jonah ran away from the Lord and headed for Tarshish…But the Lord provided a great fish to swallow Jonah, and Jonah was inside the fish three days and three nights…But I, with a song of thanksgiving, will sacrifice to you. What I have vowed I will make good. Salvation comes from the Lord. And the Lord commanded the fish, and it vomited Jonah onto dry land… Then the word of the Lord came to Jonah a second time. 'Go to the great city of Nineveh and proclaim to it the message I give you.' Jonah obeyed the word of the Lord and went to Nineveh. Now Nineveh was a very large city, it took three days to go all through it. Jonah started into the city, going a day's journey and he proclaimed; 'Forty more days and Nineveh will be destroyed.' The Ninevites believed God. They declared a fast, and all of them, from the*

⊰ Week Five: Healing from the Inside Out ⊱

STUDY APPLICATION: (Done Individually for Group Discussion)

greatest to the least, put on sackcloth...When God saw what they did and how they turned from their evil ways, He had compassion and did not bring upon them the destruction He had threatened...But Jonah was greatly displeased and became angry. He prayed to the Lord, 'O Lord, is this not what I said when I was still at home? That is why I was so quick to flee to Tarshish. I knew that you are a gracious and compassionate God, slow to anger and abounding in love, a God who relents from sending calamity. Now, O Lord, take away my life, for it is better for me to die than to live.' " —Jonah 1:1,3,17; 2:9&10; 3:1–5, 10; 4:1–3

1. Why did Jonah run away? What was he more afraid of than disobeying God?

2. God got Jonah's attention by way of the fish, and Jonah agreed to go to Nineveh. What task was he given and what was the end result supposed to be?

3. When God changed His mind why was Jonah so furious? Why does God ask us to do things that have the potential to make us look like we don't know what we're doing?

4. If God is so gracious and compassionate that He can turn from destroying a city, how does He want us to show compassion to people who don't want to engage and participate in their need situation?

5. What is the end result for any of us who choose to continue in lifestyles of sin? Is it important for us to warn people caught in sin and poor choices, even if they don't want to listen and even when we don't want to tell them? Why?

☙ Week Five: Healing from the Inside Out ❧

WEEK IN REVIEW (Indvidual/Group Activity)

Summarize each day's key concept into a short phrase.

1. _____

2. _____

3. _____

4. _____

5. _____

How have you responded (past and currently) to situations similar to what was studied this week?

Based on what you're learning, evaluate what you can change or do differently when faced with similar situations in the future.

What one thought, concept or statement has made the greatest impact on you this week?

Select one Bible verse for memorization:_____

Week Five: Healing from the Inside Out

Additional Thoughts

_____

_____

_____

_____

_____

_____

_____

_____

_____

_____

_____

_____

_____

Additional Scriptures:
Proverbs 21:5; Luke 4: 42&43, 14:27–30, 22:42; John 12:26–28; Acts 20:24; 2 Corinthians 8:11–15, 9:12&13; Galatians 4:18; Philippians 1:6, 3:7–9,12–14; Timothy 4:2&5; Hebrews 6:10; 1 Peter 3: 15&16; Jude 22

Week Five: Healing from the Inside Out

Closing Prayer

Father God, help me to be a willing servant even when the task is unpleasant and unpopular. Would I seek You humbly for direction, focusing on pleasing You, in spite of what the world may be telling me to do. Give me the ability to see the potential within others and never to do for them the things they can do for themselves. Help me to put my own motives and emotions aside as I seek to serve in ways that heal, not cripple, those around me. Give me an obedient heart, willing to do any task without a need to be a part of the harvest. Grow my faith and trust in You that I can leave others in Your hand, even when the fruit is tender and unripe. Thank you, Father, for demonstrating what a father should be, loving me as Your child, disciplining me when I need it and encouraging me when I'm down. Would my life be one of faithful obedience that glorifies You. Amen.

Week Six:
Changing the World One Life at a Time

⊰ Week Six: Changing the World One Life at a Time ⊱

Case Study Story

Crystal looked at the audience with tears running down her cheeks, her smile said it all. The applause affirmed her miraculous story. Crystal's mentor extended her hand and the two left the stage, laughing and crying at the same time. I was also touched, with tears in my eyes and a lump in my throat. A silent thank-you left my lips as I glanced up and thought the angels must be applauding too. It seemed so long ago, yet it was only ten months earlier that I met Crystal when she came into my office hoping to get matched with a mentor. She even looked different back then. She was still pretty, but walked with her head down and shoulders slumped, as if to become invisible to those around her. Her adult son belied her age, but she had several young ones still relying on her to patch their broken lives back together again. She was on the run from an abusive relationship with her third husband, the result of one of the many poor choices scattered throughout her past. The shelter had sent her to us. They could keep her safe, but they needed us to help her get back on her feet. Her answers revealed a lack of education and confidence, her sentences hesitant and disjointed. Pregnant at a young age, she had never finished school. Her past revealed her involvement with several men, all abusive, the shame reflected in her bright blue eyes. She needed employment because she knew she needed money if she wanted to become independent. In spite of how bleak it all looked, Crystal had one thing going for her—she was determined to change her life. As we started to work with her weekly, we also saw the transforming power of God at work in her. It wasn't long before the God she once had head knowledge of moved into her heart. As she grabbed onto Him for life, we witnessed His countless interventions when her volatile ex-husband unsuccessfully and repeatedly tried to hurt her. God was taking care of her needs from small to large even providing a new car from a complete stranger as she fled the state until her husband could be caught. Against all odds she found a stable job and worked hard. She was a good employee and was given a chance to advance in her position. With a lot of hard work and determination, she managed to pay off her outstanding debt, get a place of her own and start a savings account. Her children blossomed under the love and strength they saw in their

Week Six: Changing the World One Life at a Time

Case Study Story

transformed mother. Their future looked bright, so different from just one year ago. Yes, God had worked a miracle in her life and we had the privilege of being a small part of it. Crystal needed someone to give her a chance and God brought her to us. Doing Kingdom work isn't about what we can do. It's all about what He can do through us for those He sends to us.

⊰ Week Six: Changing the World One Life at a Time ⊱

Introduction

Years ago, when we first started our program, we thought we would help people pay off debt, and we have. But the transformation God has worked in each person with a willing spirit is so much more than we ever could have imagined or planned. Marriages are saved, family relationships restored, employment and housing options improved, finances stabilized, and savings accounts established. But with all of these wonderful things we see transpire in the lives of those we work with, the most life-transforming change is their relationship with God. When they start to view their life as a gift from God and manage their assets as if they were His, not theirs, everything else seems to fall into place. Nothing can compare to the experience of being used by God to touch another's life. We can't do it on our own, but with Him nothing is impossible.

> **Nothing can compare to the experience of being used by God to touch another's life.**

Week Six: Changing the World One Life at a Time

DAY ONE: Life is Hard

I have never met anyone, who if given time to share their story, hasn't shared some suffered hardship. Life is hard. I even feel that instead of life getting easier as I seek to follow Christ, it has become more challenging. Why doesn't God protect us from the difficulties, hurts and sorrows life brings to us? I've had many rough patches in my life, some of my own doing and others beyond my control. While I suffered in them, each time I worked my way out, I found myself stronger as if God used them to teach and train me. How like God to take the tragedy of sin and use it for His redeeming purposes. Trials are one of the tools He uses to reshape us into His image. Just as metal is strengthened in the fire, we too are strengthened through the trial. But what happens when people don't work their way out of a trial or challenge? Instead of being refined by their challenge they end up being confined in it. Haven't we interrupted the need for people to work their way out of difficult situations because we're too willing to feed, clothe and shelter them in their crisis? Instead of living full and productive lives, they have become stuck in an existence that God never intended for them. I believe this is what has happened to thousands of people trapped in generational poverty. Perhaps we have interfered in God's divine work of transforming grace by the way we help. What would happen if we didn't just feed people, but grabbed their hand and walked with them through the trial? Couldn't we both be transformed through the process?

Challenge: Why are hard times a part of life?

Week Six: Changing the World One Life at a Time

DAY ONE: Life is Hard

SCRIPTURE REFERENCES

"No, in all these things we are more than conquerors through Him who loved us." —Romans 8:37

"…because we know that suffering produces perseverance; perseverance, character; and character, hope." —Romans 5:3&4

"Therefore we do not lose heart. Though outwardly we are wasting away, yet inwardly we are being renewed day by day. For our light and momentary troubles are achieving for us an eternal glory that far outweighs them all." —2 Corinthians 4:16&17

"No discipline seems pleasant at the time, but painful. Later on, however, it produces a harvest of righteousness and peace for those who have been trained by it. Therefore, strengthen your feeble arms and weak knees. 'Make level paths for your feet,' so that the lame may not be disabled, but rather healed." —Hebrews 12:11&13

Life is hard, but it's not all in vain. Challenges can become opportunities for growth if we embrace them rather than try to escape them. Everything in the Bible suggests we are to persevere and be overcomers, not be overcome with hopelessness. Going through the trial is difficult, but we are called to use it as a time of training through which we should grow stronger. How much damage do we do when we help people exist in resigned complacency rather than encourage them on to victory? If we don't help them strengthen themselves and clear the path before them, don't we ultimately disable rather than heal them? Troubles can achieve divine purposes if we allow them to. Is the plan for God's transforming work being sabotaged by well-intentioned do-gooders?

Week Six: Changing the World One Life at a Time

DAY ONE: Life is Hard

Crystal's life had been hard from youth. An early, unplanned pregnancy with her abusive boyfriend seemed to set her on a path of need and destruction that she would follow for years. Her lack of a high school education, which was interrupted as she dropped out to raise her baby, complicated her ability to be self-supporting. Lacking a positive father figure, she continued to make poor choices with men. When she came to us her hard life had beaten her up almost as much as her ex-husbands. Yet Crystal had something going for her we seldom see in people in similar circumstances. She was persistent and determined to make a better life for herself and her children. It would be this drive to triumph over her challenges that would catapult her to a new and transformed life.

1. Why is it so important to work through a trial and not get stuck in it?

   So we can continue moving past it

2. If you were trying to teach your child something, but others kept doing it for them, how would you feel?

   Angry! Frustrated

3. Crystal's life was complicated by poor choices. What did she need to help her make better choices moving forward?

   Guidance, wisdom

4. How can you encourage someone who is struggling with trials?

   If they are a believer then we know God works all things out for His glory

Week Six: Changing the World One Life at a Time

DAY TWO: What's In Your Hand?

Does everyone have assets in their life? When I looked up the word 'asset' in a thesaurus, the list of synonyms included: strength, skill, talent, ability, qualification, power, blessing, and resource. It's interesting that these words represent internal qualities not external things. A speaker I once heard challenged us to look at what was in our hand and then use it in ministry. His point was that we all have something to offer. The thought that came to my mind turned that question around. Instead of just asking the giver what they have to give, shouldn't we also ask the recipient what they have to bring to the table? Doesn't it help empower someone when they are encouraged to look at their strengths and not just where they are weak? As I studied the Scriptures, I found many places in the Bible where people in need were asked what they had, not what they needed. It was as if familiar passages took on new meaning to me as I realized God likes to work His miracles through the assets people have, no matter how small or insignificant they may seem. Letting God work through what He's given someone puts the focus on Him as the provider and multiplier, not on us as the giver. I believe He still wants us involved, but does He want us to help others realize what they already have rather than just meet their need? I've asked people in difficult situations what they have to contribute and it's not easily answered. For generations they have not assessed their own assets, they have only focused on what others can give them or do for them. Do you believe everyone has something God can use to help them meet their own need? Do we need to take a closer look at what God has given us, no matter how big or small, believing He might want to work a miracle through it?

Challenge: When asked for help, why do we focus on what people need and forget to explore what they might have that could help in their situation?

Week Six: Changing the World One Life at a Time

DAY TWO: What's In Your Hand?

SCRIPTURE REFERENCES

"The wife of a man from the company of the prophets cried out to Elisha, 'Your servant my husband is dead, and you know that he revered the Lord. But now his creditor is coming to take my two boys as his slaves.' Elisha replied to her, 'How can I help you? Tell me, what do you have in your house?' 'Your servant has nothing there at all,' she said, 'except a little oil.' Elisha said, 'Go around and ask all your neighbors for empty jars. Don't ask for just a few. Then go inside and shut the door behind you and your sons. Pour oil into all the jars, and as each is filled, put it to one side.' She left him and afterward shut the door behind her and her sons. They brought the jars to her and she kept pouring. When all the jars were full she said to her son, 'Bring me another one.' But he replied, 'There is not a jar left.' Then the oil stopped flowing. She went and told the man of God, and he said, 'Go, sell the oil and pay your debts. You and your sons can live on what is left.'" —2 Kings 4:1–7

"'As surely as the Lord your God lives,' she replied, 'I don't have any bread—only a handful of flour in a jar and a little oil in a jug. I am gathering a few sticks to take home and make a meal for myself and my son, that we may eat it—and die.' Elijah said to her, 'Don't be afraid. Go home and do as you have said. But first make a small cake of bread for me from what you have and bring it to me, and then make something for yourself and your son.'"
—1 Kings 17:12&13

Throughout the Bible we see God working miracles multiplying what people have. It doesn't seem to matter how small or insignificant it is—what appears important is that we recognize what we have and are willing to release it back to God to work with. God works His miracles through what He's given us. Our needs and deficiencies mean nothing to Him. But if we can't see what we have, or won't release it, is there anything God can do? Are you clutching what's in your hand, afraid to give it up, or are you willing to surrender it, let go and let God bless it abundantly?

Week Six: Changing the World One Life at a Time

DAY TWO: What's In Your Hand?

 Crystal seemed to recognize she had assets she could bring to the table. While almost everything in her life was a mess, she knew that the future she wanted for herself and her children would only happen if she helped make it happen. She didn't come to us to see what we could give her. She came to us to see if we could help her get on her feet. She needed us, but she didn't want to be spoon-fed. She wanted us to teach her how to provide for herself and her children. She wanted to grow her assets.

1. Why do you think God sometimes works miracles with what we have and not with what others can give us?

2. What positive emotions are reinforced when we help people identify their assets?

3. What assets did Crystal have that God was using to change her life?

4. What's in your hand that God wants to work a miracle through?

Week Six: Changing the World One Life at a Time

DAY THREE: Value of Work

One of my favorite quotes comes from a man, Nick Vujicic, who has every reason to be depressed. Born without arms and legs, it appeared his life should have been sidelined since birth. But he has taken what he doesn't have and turned it into a platform to encourage others. His quote sums it up nicely, "Life without meaning has no hope. Life without hope has no faith. If you find a way to contribute, you will find your meaning, and hope and faith will naturally follow and accompany you into your future." If our meaning in life comes through how we contribute, isn't it crucial to help people engage in meaningful ways? Does giving without avenues of participation perpetuate worthlessness and dependency? One important way we contribute is through the work we do whether it is paid or voluntary. Yet it appears that the value of work has become diminished in today's society. Isn't there a lot of attention and activity focused around how we can work less and play more? Does this drive to work less actually accomplish the intended goal—do we feel more content, satisfied and fulfilled in today's culture? For many who live in continual need, going to work is a random occurrence, not a lifestyle modeled by parents to their children. Honest work restores dignity and affirms one's self-worth. My father passed a strong work ethic on to me. I find work brings me purpose and gives meaning to my life. But what if I hadn't lived in an environment where it was practiced? Would I feel differently about the value of work? Would I recognize the ability to work as a gift from God, rather than an unpleasant task I want to avoid? What happens when our helping efforts make it possible for someone to survive without contributing or working—have we stolen God's gift from them?

Challenge: Has the value of work become understated?

Week Six: Changing the World One Life at a Time

DAY THREE: Value of Work

SCRIPTURE REFERENCES

"By the seventh day God had finished the work He had been doing."
—Genesis 2:2

"I have brought you glory on earth by completing the work you gave me to do."
—John 17:4

"That every man may eat and drink, and find satisfaction in all his toil—this is the gift of God." —Ecclesiastes 3:13

"Our people must learn to devote themselves to doing what is good, in order that they may provide for daily necessities and not live unproductive lives."
—Titus 3:14

Work is biblical. In the book of Genesis we see that God worked and "saw that it was good." Jesus came to earth with a job to do and He was focused on completing it. Because we are created in His image have we not also been instilled with a natural desire to contribute through some type of meaningful work? Is it any wonder that with the huge unemployment and under-employment numbers people are depressed, despondent and disengaged? It seems people don't have to work to exist, but has this come at too great a cost? Is giving others what they need to survive, without requiring some contribution on their part, sucking the very life out of them?

Week Six: Changing the World One Life at a Time

DAY THREE: Value of Work

CASE STUDY Crystal wanted and needed to work if she was going to turn her life around. But she was under-educated and had only been able to find low paying jobs when she came to us. She needed help identifying her skills and finding a job she could be good at and feel good about. Crystal worked hard to get her GED and even harder to find a job. Once she found someone willing to take a chance on her, she exceled and was quickly promoted to better paying positions. She loved going to work because it gave her meaning and brought hope to her life. Faith naturally started to follow her into the future.

1. Why is the ability to work a gift from God?

2. What positive emotions are reinforced when we work and contribute toward our own welfare?

3. What characteristics did Crystal possess that helped make her a good employee?

4. What are some things you can do to help those who don't want to work see the value in contributing their assets?

Week Six: Changing the World One Life at a Time

DAY FOUR: An Attitude of Gratitude

Does an attitude of gratitude make a difference in our life circumstances? When times are difficult and everything seems to be falling apart, will it really make a difference if I'm thankful? Will I feel less hungry, or cold, or alone if I find something to give thanks for? Author Ann Voskamp said "Eucharisteo—thanksgiving—always precedes the miracle." If God is going to do a miracle in us or through us, do we first have to acknowledge, with thanksgiving, what we have been given? In difficult times it is hard to remember that in spite of what we currently face we have much to give thanks for. I have found that when I struggle, if I focus on the positive it changes my perspective, which has the potential to change everything. Is it possible that we can help people more effectively if we help them give thanks, no matter how small or insignificant it seems? Usually the desire to have something stems from a dissatisfaction with what we currently have. Because what we have is perceived as insufficient, it creates a need or desire to have something else and we often overlook the things we do have. Aren't many helping efforts further complicated when what we offer is not wanted, causing an expression of ingratitude instead of thankfulness? Ingratitude could be compared to wearing sunglasses in the middle of the night—it only complicates one's ability to see clearly in an already dark situation. If miracles truly do follow thanksgiving, what could happen if the "why me Lord?" turned to "thank you Lord"? Does a thankful heart create an attitude shift that has the potential to change a situation for the better?

Challenge: How much does the attitude of a person in need affect the outcome of their situation?

Week Six: Changing the World One Life at a Time

DAY FOUR: An Attitude of Gratitude

SCRIPTURE REFERENCES

"Give thanks to the Lord, for He is good; His love endures forever."
—1 Chronicles 16:34

"Let them give thanks to the Lord for His unfailing love and His wonderful deeds for men, for He satisfies the thirsty and fills the hungry with good things." —Psalm 107:8&9

"I know what it is to be in need, and I know what it is to have plenty. I have learned the secret of being content in any and every situation, whether well fed or hungry, whether living in plenty or in want." —Philippians 4:12

"But godliness with contentment is great gain. For we brought nothing into the world, and we can take nothing out of it. But if we have food and clothing, we will be content with that." —1 Timothy 6:6–8

"Be joyful always, pray continually; give thanks in all circumstances, for this is God's will for you in Christ Jesus." —1 Thessalonians 5:16–18

God has clearly instructed us to give thanks. Why is being thankful so important to Him? Could it be that it reflects the inner condition of our heart and if our heart isn't right, it's much more difficult for other things to be right? How powerful is an attitude of gratitude? Some people have so little materially and yet seem to be filled with joy and peace. Could it be that they have learned how to be content in each and every situation through an attitude of gratitude?

Week Six: Changing the World One Life at a Time

DAY FOUR: An Attitude of Gratitude

 Crystal had an attitude of gratitude from the very first time we met her. As her faith with Jesus became real and personal, her expression of thanksgiving to God was like a bubbling brook, splashing on anyone close enough to hear her. Could it have been her attitude of thanksgiving that opened her eyes and her heart to see and receive countless miracles and blessings? God delights in meeting us at our point of need, but can a thankful heart bring an even bigger blessing in the end?

1. Why is it so hard to have an attitude of gratitude when times are tough?

2. How can a thankful heart change a difficult situation?

3. How much did Crystal's attitude of gratitude affect her outcome?

4. How can we encourage a struggling individual to be thankful without appearing insensitive or rude?

Week Six: Changing the World One Life at a Time

DAY FIVE: We Are Not the Final Answer

I read once that whenever a Christian is in a position to offer advice, mentor or serve someone, they must be careful not to be the final answer. I found myself challenged by that thought—how do I help but still make sure I point them to Christ at the same time? Sometimes in our effort to relieve someone's pain we can unintentionally be seen as their savior in that particular circumstance. When they look to us for their needs and we meet the need completely, it may stop them from looking further to Christ. Shouldn't everything we do also move them one step closer to Christ? My husband has demonstrated how this works through his responses to me when I want encouragement or advice. He usually asks some challenging questions, or debates another side of the issue, stretching what I think and leaving me unsatisfied and without a final answer. While I don't initially like this process, his questions and comments always throw me into Christ's arms as I search for the answer. Any time we are in the helping business we will have opportunity to be the final answer to what someone needs. Is it important that as we meet need, give advice, or offer direction, we also point the person to Christ and His Word? A way to guard against appearing superior to those who need help is always to remember and communicate that God is the source of any strength, power and wisdom. While we can be a powerful tool God uses, we can do nothing alone. How can we serve in such a way as not to be the final answer?

> **Challenge: In what ways can we meet a person's need but also encourage them to reach out to Christ?**

⁓ Week Six: Changing the World One Life at a Time ⁓

DAY FIVE: We Are Not the Final Answer

SCRIPTURE REFERENCES

"In Lystra there sat a man crippled in his feet, who was lame from birth and had never walked. He listened to Paul as he was speaking. Paul looked directly at him, saw that he had faith to be healed and called out, 'Stand up on your feet!' At that, the man jumped up and began to walk. When the crowd saw what Paul had done, they shouted in the Lycaonian language, 'The gods have come down to us in human form!'...But when the apostles Barnabas and Paul heard of this, they tore their clothes and rushed into the crowd, shouting: 'Men, why are you doing this? We too are only men, human like you. We are bringing you good news, telling you to turn from these worthless things to the living God, who made heaven and earth and sea and everything in them.' " —Acts 14:8–11, 14&15

"To this John replied, 'A man can receive only what is given him from heaven'...He must become greater; I must become less.' " —John 3:27&30

"My message and my preaching were not with wise and persuasive words, but with a demonstration of the Spirit's power, so that your faith might not rest on men's wisdom, but on God's power." —1 Corinthians 2:4&5

The disciples were performing many miracles and it would have been easy for people to look to them instead of Christ. They modeled great humility as they eagerly and quickly exalted Christ and humanized themselves. May they serve as role models to us as we seek to help others, motivating us to serve in such a way that while we may feed them, they always leave hungry to know more of Christ.

Week Six: Changing the World One Life at a Time

DAY FIVE: We Are Not the Final Answer

 Crystal's greatest need was a restored relationship with Christ. We could help meet her physical and emotional needs, but the core, underlying spiritual need could only be answered by Christ. The transformation we witnessed in her life was not humanly possible. We were not her final answer, but we were a resource God worked through to help touch and change her forever.

1. Why do many current helping methods meet need but leave Christ out?

2. Why is it important not to be someone's final answer?

3. How would Crystal's end result have been different if Christ had been left out of the scenario?

4. What things do you need to change when responding to a person's need so they look beyond you to Christ?

Week Six: Changing the World One Life at a Time

STUDY APPLICATION: (Done Individually for Group Discussion)

Helping others is not something that should be done lightly or thoughtlessly. It can be easy to meet someone's need but ultimately interfere in the work God is doing in their life. All physical things are temporary. Only a relationship with Christ is eternal and that should be our ultimate goal—to model Christ to people in such a way they desire and come to a deeper, personal relationship with Him. So often our temporary help complicates or circumvents the process God is using to bring them into a relationship with Him. If how we meet need removes their need for Christ, what should we do? How is God calling us to do Kingdom work here on earth?

> **Sometimes the way we help can complicate or circumvent the process God is using to bring someone to Him.**

Week Six: Changing the World One Life at a Time

STUDY APPLICATION: (Done Individually for Group Discussion)

BIBLICAL STUDY

"So when the Midianite merchants came by, his brothers pulled Joseph up out of the cistern and sold him for twenty shekels of silver to the Ishmaelites, who took him to Egypt…Meanwhile, the Midianites sold Joseph in Egypt to Potiphar, one of the Pharaoh's officials, the captain of the guard… From the time he put him in charge of his household and of all that he owned, the Lord blessed the household of the Egyptian because of Joseph. The blessing of the Lord was on everything Potiphar had, both in the house and in the field…When his master heard the story his wife told him saying, 'This is how your slave treated me,' he burned with anger. Joseph's master took him and put him in prison, the place where the king's prisoners were confined. But while Joseph was there in the prison, the Lord was with him; He showed him kindness and granted him favor in the eyes of the prison warden…The chief cupbearer, however, did not remember Joseph; he forgot him…Then Pharaoh said to Joseph, 'Since God has made all this known to you, there is no one so discerning and wise as you. You shall be in charge of my palace, and all my people are to submit to your orders. Only with respect to the throne will I be greater than you.'" —Genesis 37:28, 36; 39:5, 19–21; 40:23; 41:39&40

Week Six: Changing the World One Life at a Time

STUDY APPLICATION: (Done Individually for Group Discussion)

1. Joseph had a hard life. Review the different hardships that befell him and discuss how his own actions contributed to the difficulty.

2. While Joseph could have become bitter and discouraged with the unfairness of life, he didn't. How did he respond each time he found himself in a new and difficult situation, and what was the Lord able to do through those responses?

3. How was God orchestrating each of the events in Joseph's life to position him where He needed him to be?

4. Work was an important component in both Joseph's and Crystal's lives. Talk about why it was so important to their futures.

5. For both Joseph and Crystal, their attitude played a huge role in their outcome. Talk about how things would have been different if complaining and ingratitude had become a way of life for them.

6. Try to imagine how you might have responded if you had found yourself in Joseph's or Crystal's situation. Share a time in your life when how you responded to something changed or impacted your life dramatically.

Week Six: Changing the World One Life at a Time

WEEK IN REVIEW (Indvidual/Group Activity)

Summarize each day's key concept into a short phrase.

1. _____

2. _____

3. _____

4. _____

5. _____

How have you responded (past and currently) to situations similar to what was studied this week?

Based on what you're learning, evaluate what you can change or do differently when faced with similar situations in the future.

What one thought, concept or statement has made the greatest impact on you this week?

Select one Bible verse for memorization:_____

Week Six: Changing the World One Life at a Time

Additional thoughts

Additional Scriptures:
Psalm 33:18&19, 34:6&18, 72:12, 145:14–18; Ecclesiastes 3:22; 1 Corinthians 3:9–11, 18–19; 2 Corinthians 3:5, 4:7, 5:20; Colossians 2:2&3; 1 Thessalonians 4:11&12

Week Six: Changing the World One Life at a Time

Closing Prayer

Father God, help me to see the challenges and difficult times in life as opportunities to be refined for Your divine purposes. Give me wisdom and discernment to know when and how I should respond to needs around me. Give me Your eyes to see and Your voice to speak to the lives of those I serve, helping them see their assets that You can work with. May I always encourage others in ways that allow them to contribute to their situation, helping them find meaning and purpose in their own life. Father, let me never be the final answer, but always a stepping stone to You. May I never circumvent what You are doing by offering a temporary solution that may interfere with Your eternal plan. Make me into a useful tool, not a diversion from the greater work You are doing in each of our lives. Amen.

Conclusion and Summary

Conclusion

Living out compassion in a redemptive way is challenging. Even after years of working closely with those who struggle in need and those who struggle to help them, I find I have more questions than answers. For me these answers don't come easily and are only found through the challenge of trying to do it differently. If making a defining difference in the lives of those we serve was easy, we would see it being done effectively around the world. Yet while it may be challenging, it doesn't mean it is impossible. With God's help all things are possible.

> **We can't change the world, we can only change ourselves.**

Change always starts with the individual. We can't change the world, we can only change ourselves. But if enough people believe and make a change themselves, then change within our communities, nation and the world will become a reality.

Before God can use us as a transforming change agent for others, we must become transformed within. I believe we can only live out redemptive compassion publicly after we have first wrestled with the philosophy privately. Personal conversion is a prerequisite for community transformation. Everyone has needs in their life. The degree of need and the things we need vary greatly, but each of us struggles with inadequacies and deficiencies. Recognizing our deep need for God should cause us to have an almost unquenchable thirst for His refreshing Spirit, creating a desire to drink deeply from the well of abundant and eternal life.

The goal of this study is not to bring people to a standard of life I find acceptable but to help each person achieve the fullness of life God desires for them. Putting aside our preconceived notions of what is acceptable or needed in another's life will allow us to ask God to reveal the potential buried treasure inside those we help. God alone holds the key that unlocks the mysteries hidden deep inside and we must go to Him first before we reach out to others.

Conclusion

I have come to believe dependency on God combined with an interdependence between ourselves and others is worth striving for. Finding a balance between complete dependency on others and an unhealthy self-sufficiency in ourselves can only be achieved when God is invited into the equation. God calls us to live in community with Him and others. Understanding the balance of how we relate, work, and encourage one another can create a healthy environment in which we can thrive, not just survive. Redemptive compassion that makes a defining difference in the lives of those we help is best done through a supportive community. The combined strengths of ourselves and others, braided together with our Heavenly Father creates a strand that cannot be easily broken. *"A cord of three strands is not quickly broken."* —Ecclesiastes 4:12

There are many different options that can be explored in how to implement the principles in this study guide. I know from personal experience, as the Executive Director of Love INC of Treasure Valley, that the ministry of Love In the Name of Christ is an excellent tool to be considered as you make your individual and collective decisions about how to live out redemptive compassion. Love INC's mission is to mobilize local churches to transform lives and communities in the name of Christ. I have found the unified Body of Christ to be all-inclusive with its resources, expertise, and skills. God's unified Church is the perfect tool to live out redemptive compassion in ways that will change not only the individual, but their families, the community, and our nation. Go to the Love INC movement website at loveinc.org and see if there is a Love INC Affiliate in your community or learn more about how to start one in your area.

⋈ Summary ⋈

 **Imprisoned With Kindness:**
Invest relationally in others

Life-transformation requires we look beyond the need and engage relationally with the person as we work together toward lasting solutions for their needs

Day 1:   Building relationships fosters transformation

Day 2:   We need to focus on the person not just their need

Day 3:   A hand-out meets a need while a hand-up meets the person and helps them out of need

Day 4:   Charity Compassion treats symptoms of the need not the root causes

Day 5:   Developmental Compassion is not done to or for someone but with someone

⊰ Summary ⊱

 **The Call to Love: Is It Possible?**
Require mutual contribution and participation

When addressing need, lack of planning can perpetuate self-serving giving that often cripples and imprisons those being helped, sustaining them in need, rather than freeing them from need

Day 1: Predetermined policies and plans help churches respond, not react, to requests for help

Day 2: People can become imprisoned in need, sustained by others who provide reactive, ongoing help

Day 3: Doing things for rather than with people can cripple not strengthen them

Day 4: Self-serving giving is emotionally driven. Sacrificial giving does what is needed regardless of how it feels

Day 5: Christ-like love motivates us to do the right thing because we care too much not to

Summary

WEEK THREE

Seeing Through Our Father's Eyes
See everyone's value

People are valuable to us because God created them which makes them worth our investment. How we listen, speak and respond to individuals' needs will either restore worth and hope or reinforce their negative self-image and feelings of failure

Day 1: When we recognize someone's value to God we become willing to invest in them relationally

Day 2: How we respond to need will either restore self-worth or reinforce a negative self-image

Day 3: Listening begins the relationship required to discern how to provide effective help

Day 4: Affirming words can serve as a mirror reflecting an individual's unrealized potential in Christ

Day 5: Restoring hope can reignite dreams and passions long forgotten or ignored

≼ Summary ≽

 **Tough Love for Tough Times**
Respond with discernment and wisdom

Need is complicated and multi-faceted and requires collective spiritual discernment, honesty, and wisdom to determine the correct godly response that will not promote irresponsibility or greed

Day 1: Essential life resources build on one another, but when depleted can create a domino effect of need

Day 2: Collective spiritual discernment helps determine the respective roles of God, recipient, and giver

Day 3: Extending truth and expecting honesty in a relationship communicates worth and commitment

Day 4: Saving people from the consequences of their choices teaches irresponsibility

Day 5: It is difficult to distinguish between what we want and what we really need

⊰ Summary ⊱

WEEK FIVE

Healing from the Inside Out
Help everyone achieve their God-given potential

Kingdom work takes a focused commitment regardless of how we feel about doing it or the perceived results. It's important we not absolve others from living up to their full potential and that we encourage them to accept personal responsibility for their own families

Day 1: Accomplishing Kingdom work requires a clear focus and singleness of purpose

Day 2: To the full extent possible, people need to actively engage in their own need situations

Day 3: How we respond to need is as important as if we respond—doing the right thing matters

Day 4: Providing for children's needs without engaging the parents propagates an unhealthy lifestyle

Day 5: To be obedient in God's work is more important than achieving worldly success

⁕ Summary ⁕

 **Changing the World One Life at a Time**
Serve in ways that transform

Gratefully acknowledging God's omnipotence allows Him to use the difficult times to transform us into Christ's image, working through who we are and what we have to contribute

Day 1: God uses the hard times in life to transform us

Day 2: God can take what we have and multiply it to meet our need, no matter how insignificant it may seem

Day 3: Work is a gift from God and everyone has assets to contribute

Day 4: Cultivating an attitude of gratitude can change everything

Day 5: Let us not so satisfy one's need that there is no hunger for Christ

The Wagon Principle

A component of the
Redemptive Compassion® Series

The Wagon Principle ©2013, Lois M. Tupyi, Reprint 2017
Scripture taken from the HOLY BIBLE,
NEW INTERNATIONAL VERSION.NIV.
Copyright ©1973, 1978, 1984 by International Bible Society.
Used by permission of Zondervan. All rights reserved worldwide.

Narcissa Whitman Diary: Public Domain
Excerpts of the history of Narcissa Whitman taken from:
Online Encyclopedia of Washington State History
History Link File #10088

All rights reserved. No portion of this book may be reproduced, stored in a retrieval system, or transmitted in any form or by any means—electronic, mechanical, photocopy, recording, or any other—except for brief quotations in printed reviews, without prior permission of the publisher.

The Wagon Principle

PREFACE

The Wagon Principle is a component of the Redemptive Compassion® series. This simple wagon analogy was conceived during one of my weekly discussions with staff as we talked about how we could bring clarity to the idea of wholistic help. One of the staff said, "It's kind of like a wagon. If all four wheels aren't operable, the wagon cannot move." When we try to help people wholistically, we have to look at the whole person not just their state of need or one particular need. It's a simple thought, but one that can be easily grasped and it has become a great training resource for anyone who wants to help people thrive, not merely survive, in life.

Included are excerpts from the diary of Narcissa Whitman on her trek westward in 1836 to add a real-life dimension to the piece, but there is no direct correlation between her journey and the wagon analogy.

The Wagon Principle is one component in Redemptive Compassion, and is based on the biblical philosophy that we can help people in ways that move them out of need and into the fullness of life that God has promised to all. I recommend that you visit the redemptivecompassion.org website to learn more about all the training pieces available through Redemptive Compassion.

Personal transformation cannot be done for *someone, but* with *someone and through the help of God.*

The Wagon Principle

HOPE FOR A BETTER LIFE

Something ignited a deep desire within the hearts of those who embarked on the Oregon Trail. Change is usually fueled by dissatisfaction with what is while looking forward to what could be.

Redemptive Compassion—help that frees—is a process similar to the journey emigrants took westward in their quest for a new and better life. Those embarking on the journey were motivated for different reasons but all had one final hope in mind—a better life filled with new opportunities.

People are motivated by a multitude of different reasons when seeking help. Sadly, most of them have lost hope for a better life and are focused solely on someone meeting an immediate need with an often temporary fix.

Offering redemptive compassion is a wholistic approach to the individual in need and requires a belief by those assisting that what is currently being done is not enough. This type of all-inclusive help can be challenging for the giver to extend because it is often not sought out or embraced initially by the one needing assistance, and requires an investment of time and relationship by all involved. Unless one believes that help in any other fashion will not free or transform, the journey can feel too overwhelming to even begin.

Not everyone who embarked on the journey westward arrived at their final destination. Choices and decisions made each step of the way affected the final outcome. As we step out to wholistically help others, it is important to remember that those we assist have a voice and will make choices and decisions along the way that may jeopardize their success.

The Wagon Principle

NARCISSA WHITMAN

Narcissa Whitman was the first European-American woman to cross the Rocky Mountains in 1836 on her way to found the Protestant Whitman Mission with her husband Dr. Marcus Whitman near modern day Walla Walla, Washington. They headed west for the Oregon Country in March 1836 and arrived on September 1, 1836 at Walla Walla Fort. Included are some excerpts from her diary as she made the difficult trek westward.

"Do not conform any longer to the pattern of this world, but be transformed by the renewing of your mind. Then you will be able to test and approve what God's will is— his good, pleasing and perfect will."

—Romans 12:2

The Wagon Principle

" The rest of us have been very well, except feeling the effects of drinking the river water. I am in exception, however. My health was never better than since I have been on the river. I was weighed last week, and came up to 136 pounds. I think I shall endure the journey well—perhaps better than any of the rest of us."

–Narcissa Whitman

"All Scripture is God-breathed and is useful for teaching, rebuking, correcting and training in righteousness, so that the man of God may be thoroughly equipped for every good work."

—2 Timothy 3:16&17

The Wagon Principle

THE WAGON'S UNDERCARRIAGE

A wagon's undercarriage has to be strong yet maneuverable and is the framework the bed sits on and to which the wheels attach. The key to its mobility is an iron or steel kingpin which allows the wagon to turn.

Everyone has some foundation on which they have built their life. Determining the health and strength of that framework is critical in understanding whether they will have the ability to endure the hard and strenuous journey of transformation.

Christian wholistic help is built on the strong foundation of Jesus Christ and the kingpin is the Word of God. Even if the person asking for help has no awareness or reference point of Jesus Christ, it is important to share and use God's Word as the center point from which all of our work flows. His Word:

✢ Is the lamp that lights the path

✢ Has the answers and solutions for every situation

✢ Is trustworthy in dealing with all problems

✢ Will reveal and confirm God's will through the Holy Spirit

✢ Motivates us, out of love, to align our help with His will

✢ Exposes and addresses the idols of the heart, forcing one to see those things we cling to or rely on which have not and cannot produce the desired results

The Wagon Principle

DIARY: JUNE 3ʳᴰ

"The Fur Company have seven wagons drawn by six mules each, heavily loaded, and one cart drawn by two mules, which carries a lame man, one of the proprietors of the Company. We have two wagons in our company...If you want to see the camp in motion, look away ahead and see first the pilot and the captain, Fitzpatrick, just before him, next the pack animals, all mules, loaded with great packs; soon after you will see the wagons, and in the rear, our company. We all cover quite a space."

–Narcissa Whitman

"Therefore we do not lose heart. Though outwardly we are wasting away, yet inwardly we are being renewed day by day. For our light and momentary troubles are achieving for us an eternal glory that far outweighs them all."

—2 Corinthians 4:16&17

The Wagon Principle

THE WAGON WHEEL

The wagon wheels were uniquely designed to carry the wagon bed which contained all the possessions taken with the pioneers on the journey. They were specifically designed to endure the harsh conditions and difficult terrain they would encounter. The large wheels helped the wagon roll easily over bumps and dips. The wide rims helped keep the wagon from sinking into soft ground. The front wheels were smaller than the rear wheels to permit sharp turns. At the center of each wheel was the hub and axle from which spokes flared outward attaching to the rim which was encased in iron for strength. All the wagon wheels had to be functional and working for the wagon to roll forward easily.

Wholistic help recognizes there are four wheels that affect any person's life, and to help someone move forward, all four wheels need to be examined and put in working condition. If any of the wheels are broken, misshapen or missing, it will be nearly impossible to move into the full and productive life God has planned.

The center of each wheel, the hub, must be God, with all activity, thoughts and behaviors radiating out from Him. Boundaries and accountability provided by a mentor or counselor represent the iron rim which helps the wheel stay balanced so it can roll properly.

The Wagon Principle

DIARY: JULY 25TH

"Husband has had a tedious time with the wagon to-day. It got stuck in the creek this morning when crossing, and he was obliged to wade considerably in getting it out. After that, in going between the mountains, on the side of one, so steep that it was difficult for horses pass, the wagon was upset twice; did not wonder at this at all; it was a greater wonder that it was not turning somersaults continually. It is not very grateful to my feelings to see him wearing out with such excessive fatigue, as I am obliged to. He is not as fleshy as he was last winter."

–Narcissa Whitman

But seek first his kingdom and his righteousness, and all these things will be given to you as well."

—Matthew 6:33

The Wagon Principle

THE SPIRITUAL WHEEL

The Spiritual Wheel recognizes that everyone has some belief system that guides their lives. To offer wholistic help using God and His Word as the center point, it is important to understand what the person believes and why. Some suggested questions that help understand the spokes of this wheel are:

- Do they have a belief and if so what is it?

- What has been their experience with religion in the past?

- Do they have a personal relationship with Christ or do they worship other gods?

- Does their day-to-day walk include a spiritual dimension and what does it look like?

- Do they believe in a higher power or do they believe their life is dictated by fate?

- Have they been hurt by religion and do not want anything to do with it?

- Where have they worshiped or gone to church in the past?

- Do they say their faith is active and how do they describe it?

- Do they find prayer and Scripture offensive or affirming?

- Do they use their faith as an excuse to not address other things?

The Wagon Principle

DIARY: JULY 28TH

"Very mountainous all the way to-day; came over another ridge; rode from 8 A.M. to 2 P.M. We thought yesterday the Indians were all going to leave us, except two or three; but not one has… One of the axle-trees of the wagon broke today; was a little rejoiced, for we were in hopes they would leave it, and have no more trouble with it. Our rejoicing was in vain for they are making a cart of the back wheels, this afternoon, and lashing the fore wheels to it—intending to take it through in some shape or other. They are so resolute and untiring in their efforts they will probably succeed."

–Narcissa Whitman

"So do not worry, saying, 'What shall we eat?' or 'What shall we drink?' or 'What shall we wear?' For the pagans run after all these things, and your heavenly Father knows that you need them."

—Matthew 6:31&32

The Wagon Principle

THE PHYSICAL / MATERIAL WHEEL

The Physical/Material Wheel focuses on physical needs and the material world one lives in. Physical needs are the most common type of requests made and met, e.g., food, clothing, housing, money, transportation, etc. Physical needs are easy to identify and understand. They can often be met with some type of product or money distribution, thus allowing the giver and the recipient to feel a level of immediate satisfaction that can circumvent the necessity of delving into the more complex and personal wheels. One could compare it to a wagon wheel that falls off or breaks in half—it's obvious it needs attention and fixing. All focus tends to shift to the broken wheel, and other wheels, which are also in need of repair, may get overlooked. Some suggested questions that help understand the spokes of this wheel are:

✢ What basic physical needs does the person have?

✢ Is living in need and relying on others for assistance a lifestyle and, if so, for how long?

✢ What restrictions or lack of resources are complicated by their home or work environment?

✢ What is their work history?

✢ How often do they seek help for physical/material needs?

The Wagon Principle

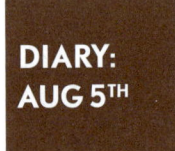
DIARY: AUG 5TH

"Mr. McLeod and his company started earlier than we did, intending to come but a little way. We could not get ready to come with him, and the man who piloted us led us wrong—much out of the way. Those on whom we depended to drive cattle disappointed us. Husband and myself fell in behind them to assist John Alts, who was all alone with them. This made us later into camp than the rest of our company. We came through several mosquitoes as to be scarcely able to see."

–Narcissa Whitman

"Therefore encourage one another and build each other up, just as in fact you are doing."

—1 Thessalonians 5:11

The Wagon Principle

THE RELATIONAL / SOCIAL WHEEL

The Relational/Social Wheel recognizes that there are outside influences that have greatly shaped who a person is and how they behave. It's critical to understand not only who has served as role models and mentors in the past, but also who is currently influencing the decisions being made. Without a good understanding of what and who has influenced the past and is currently influencing the present, the future will be difficult to change. Some suggested questions that help understand the spokes of this wheel are:

✢ Who has been or currently serves as their role model?

✢ Who do they try to please and why?

✢ Who has the greatest influence over the decisions they make?

✢ Are they in a relationship that is in crisis or is failing?

✢ Have they experienced abuse in any form in the past and have they taken any steps to heal or overcome it?

✢ Who is their current support system?

✢ What is their family history and are they in touch or estranged from them currently?

✢ How much has their use of social media influenced who they are?

✢ Who would they call in a crisis?

The Wagon Principle

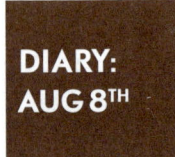

"Monday—Snake river. We have an excellent camp ground tonight; plenty of feed for our horses and cattle. We think it remarkable that suckling calves that appear to be in very good spirits; they suffer some from sore feet—otherwise they have come on well and will go through. Have come eighteen miles to-day and have taken it so deliberately that it has been easy for us."

–Narcissa Whitman

"Praise be to the God and Father of our Lord Jesus Christ, the Father of compassion and the God of all comfort, who comforts us in all our troubles, so that we can comfort those in any trouble with the comfort we ourselves have received from God."

—2 Corinthians 1:3&4

The Wagon Principle

THE EMOTIONAL / SELF WHEEL

The Emotional/Self Wheel is probably the most difficult wheel to understand. This wheel contains the attitudes, addictions, habits, self-worth, love or hate within a person. Most people work hard to conceal and pretend that this wheel is fully functioning even when it is not. The damage to this wheel may not be readily distinguishable and yet, if unaddressed, can and usually does prohibit much forward movement. Often when attempts are made to repair or strengthen the spokes of this wheel, the person will quit, become defensive or withdraw rather than face the hard work required to get the wheel up and running. Some suggested questions that help understand the spokes of this wheel are:

✣ Are they physically struggling with bad health?

✣ Do they suffer from depression, bi-polar, schizophrenia or other mental or emotional issues which make it hard to function?

✣ Do they have any addictions, compulsions or habits which negatively affect their life or others?

✣ How do they view themselves—do they have a poor self-image?

✣ Do they have the victim mentality and feel little responsibility to be an active participant of change?

✣ Do they use mental or emotional reasons as an excuse for poor behavior?

The Wagon Principle

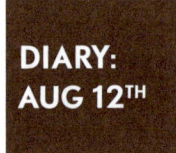

DIARY: AUG 12TH

"Dear Harriet, the little trunk you gave me has come with me so far, and now I must leave it here alone. Poor little trunk, I am sorry to leave thee; though must abide here alone, and no more by thy presence remind me of my dear Harriet. Twenty miles below the falls on Snake river this shall be thy place of rest... Thus we scatter as we go along. The hills are so steep and rocky that husband thought it best to lighten the wagon as much as possible and take nothing but the wheels."

–Narcissa Whitman

"Do not store up for yourselves treasures on earth, where moth and rust destroy, and where thieves break in and steal. But store up for yourselves treasures in heaven, where moth and rust do not destroy, and where thieves do not break in and steal. For where your treasure is, there your heart will be also."

—Matthew 6:19-21

The Wagon Principle

THE WAGON BOX

The wagon box carried everything necessary to make the journey and start a new life. It was carefully packed to keep the center of gravity low and to avoid puncturing the cover—heavy things on the bottom and layered upward with the lightest things on top. Most wagons were uncomfortable to ride in, lacking springs and packed tightly, so the emigrants normally walked or rode beside it as they journeyed.

In wholistic help, the wagon box contains the things that fill one's life. As individuals agree to start on a journey to life-transformation, everything packed into their life will need to be examined for worth and necessity—forcing hard decisions as needs versus wants are examined and agonized over to seek balance through established boundaries.

Normally, the longer the journey and the steeper the terrain, more and more of what was thought to be essential was tossed out and left behind. Many things that are initially treasured and valued will be found to be burdensome and heavy the further they journey. Eventually, these things will be replaced with the important things of life that truly embrace the full life God has promised.

The Wagon Principle

DIARY: AUG 21ˢᵀ

"Sabbath. Rich with heavenly blessings has the day of rest been to my soul. M. Spalding was invited to preach in the Fort at 11 o'clock. The theme was the character of the blessed Savior. All listened with good attention."

–Narcissa Whitman

"And pray in the Spirit on all occasions with all kinds of prayers and requests. With this in mind, be alert and always keep on praying for all the saints."

—Ephesians 6:18

The Wagon Principle

THE WAGON COVERING

The cloth top that covered the wagon had the primary purpose of providing protection for the people and their possessions stored inside. It was stretched tightly across a frame of hickory bows and could be rolled back for ventilation. The heavy canvas was often waterproofed with paint or linseed oil to prevent the elements from seeping through to what was inside the box.

Determining what serves as protection in a person's life, or if they are uncovered and exposed to all the elements, will help bring clarity to those assisting them. Prayer is the covering that needs to be stretched across all wholistic attempts to help others. Without prayer, the journey to life-transformation will feel almost unbearable as everything is subjected to the storms of life.

Prayer will release the oil of the Holy Spirit that is necessary to persevere when the journey gets steep and difficult. It will waterproof against discouragement, weariness or fear as trials and difficulties rain down.

Prayer will provide the ventilation necessary to keep conversations and relationships from over-heating and destroying the progress made or jeopardizing the journey's outcome.

The Wagon Principle

"On account of our worn out cattle and horses, it was thought best to separate from Mr. McLeod's party, at least some of us, and travel more deliberately. Two mules and a horse have almost entirely given out. It is necessary that some of our party go to Vancouver immediately for supplies and see Mr. Parker before he leaves."

–Narcissa Whitman

"Now you are the body of Christ, and each one of you is a part of it. And in the church God has appointed first of all apostles, second prophets, third teachers, then workers of miracles, also those having gifts of healing, those able to help others, those with gifts of administration, and those speaking in different kinds of tongues."

—1 Corinthians 12:27&28

The Wagon Principle

THE WAGON TRAIN

The journey to a new life was not done in isolation. Families would join others and together a caravan of wagons would form, making up what was commonly called a wagon train. There were many benefits to traveling in numbers as they supported, protected and encouraged each other along the way.

Wholistic help is difficult to do alone and is best accomplished when a community of believers comes together, each one bringing their different strengths and expertise to the effort. Together they can offer support, wisdom and direction, making it possible to endure the long journey without wearing out.

Having the benefit of a community focus on an individual's situation means that one person will not be required to meet all the different needs represented by the four wheels. Appropriate roles will be given, using different skills and resources found in the community, meeting the varied needs within an individual's life. Defining roles and boundaries with clear expectations will allow many people to share in the burden of helping someone journey to a new place in life.

The Wagon Principle

"Before noon we began to descend one of the most terrible mountains for steepness and length I have yet seen. It was like winding stairs in its descent, and in some places almost perpendicular. The horses appeared to dread the hill as much as we did. They would turn and wind around in a zigzag manner all the way down. The men usually walked, but I could not get permission to, neither did I desire it much."

–Narcissa Whitman

"Remind the people to be subject to rulers and authorities, to be obedient, to be ready to do whatever is good, to slander no one, to be peaceable and considerate, and to show true humility toward all men."

—Titus 3:1&2

The Wagon Principle

LEADING THE WAY

A caravan of wagons did not venture out without securing a captain or wagon master who would lead the caravan, helping them cross the rugged terrain and making critical decisions along the way. Scouts or  trail guides, familiar with the frontier, would be employed to work with the captain guiding them on the best routes, knowing where to ford the rivers, which passes to use when crossing the mountains, and how to avoid or get along with the Indians they would encounter. The lives of everyone on the wagon train were in the hands of those leading the way, but sometimes individuals would decide to go it alone and leave the train, often resulting in a failed attempt, and even death.

Leadership is critical when offering wholistic help, especially as a community of believers comes together with differing roles and ideas. The leader will cast the vision of what a new life can look like, keeping everyone moving in the same direction by providing the expertise, discernment and knowledge necessary to get there. Counselors, mentors and others will work closely with the leader to provide guidance and accountability to those seeking help. Some people will not like taking direction from others and will quit or go out on their own, resulting in little to no life change as they return to what they knew before beginning the journey.

The Wagon Principle

DIARY: AUG 31ST

"Came to the Walla Walla river, within eight miles of the Fort (Wallula). Husband and I were very much exhausted with this day's lengthy ride. Most of the way was sandy with not water for many miles. When we left Mr. Spalding husband rode an Indian horse when he had never mounted before and found him a hard rider in every gait except a gallop, and slow in his movements, nor could he pace as mine did, so for the last six days we have galloped most of the way where the ground would admit of it."

–Narcissa Whitman

"Let us not become weary in doing good, for at the proper time we will reap a harvest if we do not give up. Therefore, as we have opportunity, let us do good to all people, especially to those who belong to the family of believers."

—Galatians 6:9&10

The Wagon Principle

PULLING THE WAGON FORWARD

Wagons cannot move under their own power, they must be pulled. An estimated seventy percent of the wagons traveling west were pulled by oxen even though they were slower than mule or horse teams. There was a multitude of benefits in using an oxen team and chances of arriving at the final destination greatly increased, in spite of the slower and often cumbersome journey they created.

When attempting to help someone, there are several methods that can be employed, many of them more appealing and seemingly faster than the one recommended here. But we have found that yoking together the six Core Principles found in Redemptive Compassion® will provide the strength, uniformity and endurance needed for transformation. Together these six principles can move others toward the life God has planned.

- See everyone's value
- Invest relationally in others
- Help everyone achieve their God-given potential
- Require mutual contribution and participation
- Respond with discernment and wisdom
- Serve in ways that transform

The Wagon Principle

DIARY: SEPT 3RD

"About noon Mr. and Mrs. Spalding arrived with their company, having made better progress than was anticipated. Here we are all at Walla Walla, through the mercy of a kind providence, in health and all our lives preserved. What cause for gratitude and praise to God! Surely my heart is ready to leap for joy at the thought of being so near the long-desired work of teaching the benighted ones the knowledge of a Savior, and have completed this hazardous journey under such favorable circumstances."

–Narcissa Whitman

"When I was a child, I talked like a child, I thought like a child, I reasoned like a child. When I became a man, I put childish ways behind me."

—1 Corinthians 13:11

The Wagon Principle

STAGES IN THE JOURNEY

Any life-changing journey requires preparation, planning and effort. Often individuals would idealistically dream of a better life out West, not realistically considering what it was going to take to make the journey. Focused on what they thought life could be, they were unaware of how much effort it would require of them and how difficult it was going to be. Many did not make the journey, dying along the way or giving up midway and turning back to settle for a mundane existence in less than ideal circumstances.

Wholistic help is also offered in stages, each step being critical for overall success in helping the recipient reach their goals. It's important to do each stage in the right order to build the strength, capacity and commitment needed to endure the long journey ahead. Too often both the giver and the recipient focus on just one broken wheel, ignoring or jumping over all the other components necessary for a permanent change to take place.

The relationship between the giver and the recipient changes with each stage and it's critical that everyone understands their role at any given point. Doing too much will potentially cripple the recipient and destroy the outcome.

The Wagon Principle

STAGE ONE: Engage the Head

A vision is conceived by one individual who then has the task of convincing others that what they want is a good idea. I can envision a father sharing the stories he has heard of living out West with his wife and children; dreaming of a better life; detailing why they should go and sharing what he hopes for once they will arrive. Questions would be asked and together they would discuss the pros and cons of how it would affect their lives if they went. It was critical to take time to discuss things in depth and to consider all the factors that would impact the end result so they could make the best decision possible.

When someone calls or asks for help, it is important to hear their story, understand their dreams and perceived needs, and learn why they believe they need help before responding to their request. Focus is placed on the person, not on what they want, and further questions are asked to clearly discern what, if anything, one should do for them. Recognizing that all four wheels are affecting their situation means time must be taken to begin exploring the condition of each wheel as well as planting the beginning seeds of hope, value and worth.

Before the next stage begins, the six core principles must be expressed and yoked together so when the next move is determined everyone understands they have a part to play.

The Wagon Principle

STAGE TWO: Engage the Heart

Once the decision was made to go West, the second stage was entered into as the emigrants began the huge task of getting ready for the journey. Plans were made, supplies were gathered, their physical, mental and emotional health were prepared and strengthened so they could endure the difficult road ahead. No one could do this stage for them—they had to want the new life enough that they were willing to do the hard work necessary to get prepared for it.

In the second stage of wholistic help, the one helping shifts focus as they begin the process of assessing the capacity and potential of the recipient to engage and participate in their own need situation. The helper moves from asking "what is their real need and what should I do" to "what can and should they do" to help achieve their goals. This shift is often not readily embraced by the recipient, but is important because transformation is personal and individual. Only when someone has a strong desire to change and is willing to participate will God be able to work His transforming grace in and through their lives.

It is critical to employ all the wagon principles in the second stage. An understanding of the recipient's capacity can best be obtained by examining the condition of the four wheels to help identify what needs to be repaired, strengthened or replaced as they prepare to move toward the full life God has for them.

The Wagon Principle

STAGE THREE: Engage the Hands and Feet

Once the emigrants began the actual journey, they entered this final stage and it usually continued until they reached their destination. As they joined a caravan of wagons, there was mutual excitement and engagement by all as they set out together to achieve their dreams.

The third stage of wholistic help makes another shift as the one helping moves from "what can and should they do" to "what can we do working together" as both engage in the journey. That being said, the roles are not identical. The one helping serves as a counselor or guide, keeping the recipient focused on their goals by giving wise counsel and providing the accountability necessary to keep them moving forward. If at any time the recipient disengages, wanting others to do it for them, the one helping will pull back until they re-engage.

At this stage there is full disclosure on the condition of the wheels, the hidden as well as the obvious. A relationship built on trust has begun to develop with shared honesty, openness and truthfulness. Some of the more difficult repairs to the wheels are now being talked about with possible outside resources being identified to help the recipient achieve the transformed life they desire. Compassion and tough love are exhibited and practiced regularly.

This stage normally lasts until the journey is complete and the participant's goals are reached or it becomes very apparent they will be able to achieve success on their own.

The Wagon Principle

SUMMARY OF THE MAP TO SUCCESS

The journey West was a long process that took months to complete. Wholistic help is also a long process that requires a willingness to enter into a relationship and persevere through to transformation.

Use the right map:

- Use God's Word as your compass and cover everything in prayer
- Study Redemptive Compassion to understand the philosophy behind wholistic help
- Employ the six principles found in Redemptive Compassion®

Follow the map when asked for help:

Head: Listen to the story of the person requesting help to better understand their complete situation— **"What do you need and why?"**

- Ask simple questions about all four wheels
- Plant seeds of worth, potential and hope

Heart: Identify what the recipient needs to do and see if they are willing to engage— **"What can you do to get what you want?"**

- Ask additional questions about all four wheels helping them understand their own motivation for seeking help
- Identify specific goals and see if they are willing to work towards accomplishing them

Hands and Feet: Once they are actively participating, join them— **"What can we do together to reach your goals?"**

- Ask deep questions about all four wheels and discern resources that can help restore and fix what needs help
- Never do anything they can and should do for themselves
- Journey with them until they arrive or can go it alone

Narcissa found it hard to reconcile the reality of the life she lived with the one she had envisioned, back in Prattsburg. She had imagined herself living among attentive, well-behaved 'dear heathen' who would be eager to master fine points of religious doctrine, undergo and participate in spiritual conversion, take up farming, and adopt the customs and behavior of Christians like herself. She was repelled by the Indians she actually encountered. She thought they were dirty, lazy, and sinful. They ignored her standards of privacy and cleanliness. Had she been more flexible, more willing to meet the Cayuse on their own terms, to speak their language, enter their lodges, accept them into her own world—she might not have ended up being brutally beaten and dumped in the mud to die. Nothing in her background had prepared her for the cultural adaptability she needed to succeed as a missionary.

○

The Wagon Principle

A TRANSFORMED LIFE

The trek westward was long and arduous and many were disenchanted once they arrived. The journey seemed to either strengthen them for their new life or take everything out of them, leaving them depleted and depressed. The difference seemed to be rooted in the initial motives for going and their perspective once they arrived. If their motives were misplaced to begin with, there was a strong chance their perspective would be skewed when they arrived.

The same thing can happen when one tries to offer wholistic help to someone. If the one helping wants something the recipient doesn't, even if you somehow help them achieve it, chances are they'll be disappointed.

Only God can work His transforming grace in anyone. Without Him, any change will be minimal and short-lived. This is why it is so critical that prayer and God's Word guide everything said or done. Redemptive Compassion's six principles will keep us centered on Him as we seek to help others.

Summary Statement:

When we value others because God does, we become willing to invest in them relationally. Relying upon wisdom and discernment, we should then seek to help them develop to their full potential believing that mutual participation and contribution are critical in achieving a transformed life.

The Wagon Principle

A PICTORIAL DESCRIPTION

The wagon covering is prayer

Emotional/Self Wheel

Physical/Material Wheel

Spiritual Wheel

Relational/Social Wheel

The wagon box is the stuff of life that takes our time, energy and resources.

The undercarriage is Jesus Christ

In Closing

The Wagon Principle

TESTIMONIALS

"*The Wagon Principle is a refreshing, innovative, and practical way to look at the way we assess needs in our ministry. We use it as a compass for asking tough questions and the Scriptures as a map to help guide us with each and every client through the tough journey on their way to transformation. I highly recommend all people seeking to help someone, whether through a structured entity or on your own, read and study this guide.*"

– Dana Parker, Director of Love INC of the Heart of Florida

"*Lois Tupyi, in her book The Wagon Principle, has expressed some of the finest, most concise thoughts on how to truly help individuals in need become independent and productive.*"

– Steven Thayn, Idaho State Senator

"Many of our local church leadership teams have been going through the Redemptive Compassion® Study. One gentleman commented, 'I am 64 years old. I have been a Christian most of my life, but this is the first time I truly understand what "help" looks like from a biblical perspective. Now I can't wait to put what I have learned into action.' The Wagon Principle helps Christian volunteers put all they have learned about redemptive compassion into action. I highly recommend the entire Redemptive Compassion® Series to anyone desiring to help people realize their giftedness, value, and worth in Jesus Christ."

—Michele Zimmerman, Director of Love INC of Newaygo County

⊰ About the Author ⊱

Lois Tupyi is the Executive Director of Love INC of Treasure Valley. She has worked with the Canyon County based affiliate since April, 1999, when she served as its first Clearinghouse Coordinator. She accepted the responsibility of Executive Director in January 2002, and has led the local non-profit organization since then.

In 2005, Lois was asked to become a trainer for the National Love INC organization. In this capacity she has coordinated and led large group trainings locally and nationally to meet the training needs of developing affiliates. In 2011 she joined the National Love INC board for a brief time giving input on the restructure of the Love INC Movement.

Love INC of Treasure Valley's campus is a training site for people in all stages of their Love INC Ministry growth as well as others interested in learning more about Redemptive Compassion. Lois is an inspiring speaker and educator at area churches and communities across the nation, frequently traveling to share her passion for the biblical call to wholistic help.

Lois is the author of the bestseller, *Selah: Pause and Consider.* Her unique devotional encourages personal worship and spiritual growth through daily Bible reading, praise music, and beautiful photography.

Lois is an Idaho native. She and her husband currently reside on a small Hereford ranch in Wilder, where they enjoy the rural lifestyle. She has three adult children and fourteen beautiful grandchildren.

Go to the website redemptivecompassion.org to learn more about all of the Redemptive Compassion components, including video excerpts from the training DVDs. Email redemptivecompassion@gmail.com for information on how to bring Lois to your community or additional classroom training opportunities with her.

"What I do you cannot do; but what you do, I cannot do. The needs are great, and none of us, including me, ever do great things. But we can all do small things, with great love, and together we can do something wonderful."

—Mother Teresa of Calcutta